TRUE ROOTS

TRUE ROOTS

A Mindful Kitchen with
More Than 100 Recipes Free of
Gluten, Dairy, and Refined Sugar

KRISTIN CAVALLARI

with Mike Kubiesa

RODALE.

RODALE *wellness*

Live happy. Be healthy. Get inspired.

Sign up today to get exclusive access to our authors, exclusive bonuses,
and the most authoritative, useful, and cutting-edge information on health,
wellness, fitness, and living your life to the fullest.

Visit us online at RodaleWellness.com
Join us at RodaleWellness.com/Join

Rodale books may be purchased for business or promotional use or for special sales.
For information, please e-mail: BookMarketing@Rodale.com.

Printed in China
Rodale Inc. makes every effort to use acid-free ♾, recycled paper ♻.

Food photography by Tina Rupp
Food styling by Carrie Purcell
Prop styling by Stephanie Hanes
Lifestyle photography by Kelsey Cherry
Food and prop styling by Hannah Messinger
Photograph of Mike Kubiesa on page xi by Kyle Cummins

Book design by Rae Ann Spitzenberger

Library of Congress Cataloging-in-Publication Data is on file with the publisher.

ISBN 978-1-62336-916-3   paperback
ISBN 978-1-63565-279-6   signed paperback

Distributed to the trade by Macmillan

2   4   6   8   10   9   7   5   3   1   paperback

RODALE.

We inspire health, healing, happiness, and love in the world.
Starting with you.

For Jay, Camden, Jaxon, and Saylor:
My light, my love, and my inspiration.

CONTENTS

INTRODUCTION

80/20

Why? That was the question I kept asking myself when I sat down to write this introduction. Why am I writing this cookbook? And what do I want my message to be? Well, it's simple: I want everyone to be able to enjoy good food and feel well. And more than just enjoy food, I want everyone to have a great relationship with it.

In my twenties, I struggled for years to have a healthy relationship with food. I never looked at food as something to enjoy without having any feelings of guilt or regret. When it came to eating, I never felt free, and I sure as hell didn't think food had an impact on my mood. Boy, was I wrong.

The word *diet* sabotaged me from the beginning. In my early twenties, I was on a "diet" every week, and as soon as that word entered my head, I was already craving all the things I wasn't allowing myself. It was a tumultuous mental game that ultimately turned into my diet being "all or nothing" (abstaining or bingeing). I became obsessed with food, to the point where it consumed most of my thoughts, and I always felt trapped and weighed down by the guilt and shame that came from indulging.

Around age 25, I accepted a new way of eating. It was a new *lifestyle* rather than a diet, and suddenly everything else fell into place. When I decided that the "no" list would be a "not as much" list, I didn't crave anything. When I had a burger with fries dipped in ranch, then went home and ate a healthy dinner of fish and veggies, I all of a sudden had a very free relationship with food. I was no longer obsessing over it and driving myself crazy. Luckily I can thank my first pregnancy for jump-starting my journey to health.

I found that by eating healthy most of the time, when I allowed myself to indulge—when eating out or just once in a blue moon—I actually *wanted* to get back on track and eat healthy again. Because here's the secret: When you consistently eat clean, you start to feel *really* good (improved energy; clear, bright skin). I felt the best I ever had, and when I ate like crap, I didn't feel so hot and I didn't like that feeling one bit.

I started to eat healthy when I was home, and for me that was a majority of the time. When I went out to eat about once or twice a week, I ordered whatever I wanted, maybe even had a drink or two, then came home and got back on track. No guilt. No shame. No regrets. I started to notice this way of eating was releasing me of my toxic thoughts surrounding food, and I was a much happier person. Without knowing it at the time, I had developed what I now call my "80/20 lifestyle."

So what does it mean? Simply put, it means that 80 percent of the time, I eat exactly like the recipes you'll see in this cookbook, and the other 20 percent, I eat whatever I want. The key for the 80 percent is eating *real* food: grass-fed meats, wild-caught fish, organic as often as possible, and only minimally processed foods. I want my food as close to its natural state as possible.

With the 80/20 lifestyle, I started to notice that my energy improved, my skin was the best it had ever been, I was sleeping like a baby, and I hardly ever got sick. Plus, I was eating the most food I had in years—and that was reason enough for me.

Not only do I want you to feel amazing and have a healthy relationship with food, I want the experience to be fun and enjoyable, which ultimately means being realistic. Eating clean doesn't have to be difficult. It doesn't mean you have to be slaving away in the kitchen for hours, and it sure doesn't mean you're locked into only a handful of recipes (because that would be boring). It's very possible to create delicious, healthy meals and snacks in a pinch, under 30 minutes, or when you are in a cooking rut.

I want to erase the stigma that being healthy equals boring and makes you miss out on life. It's quite the opposite! Life is to be enjoyed, and good food is a crucial aspect of that. So even if you don't follow this cookbook as religiously as I do, if you want some easy-to-prep healthy meals or are just beginning your journey to healthy eating, you can have peace of mind knowing you've made the right choice to buy a book that's full of delicious, good-for-you meals.

Take it easy on yourself. Don't waste precious time and energy on negative, unnecessary thoughts surrounding food. Stay true to yourself by being kind. And don't take good health for granted; without it, we have nothing.

MY RUSTIC JOURNEY

Simple and rustic. Whenever I am preparing a dish, that's always at the core of my cooking philosophy. My food style is a balance between traditional French and Mediterranean with a modern American twist. I enjoy cooking with fresh, natural ingredients, often using vegetables grown from my own garden. My love for cooking began with family; some of my fondest childhood memories are of time spent in the kitchen with Mom and Grandma. I've always known that my love for cooking would lead to a career in the kitchen.

I was first introduced to Kristin and her husband, Jay Cutler, when I was working in the kitchen for the Chicago Bears. After their daughter, Saylor, was born, I came in and helped Kristin with meals since she now had 3 young kids to look after. Kristin and I would talk about food, and her passion for cooking was evident. She brought me in for many cooking lessons, as she wanted to learn new techniques and further her cooking skills. We started to collaborate on recipes, and that led to conversations around a cookbook–a dream we both shared. I'm honored to be a part of this book.

All of the recipes here come from the heart, with personal touches from both Kristin and me. Every recipe is a dish that we enjoy, and we are thrilled to share them with others.

Michael Kulwisa

IN THE PANTRY

IN THE FRIDGE

Apple cider vinegar: I cook and bake with this often, but more importantly, it cures just about everything. It's loaded with enzymes and potassium, and I take a shot regularly to help with heartburn and bloat, to keep colds at bay, and to maintain clear skin.

Fish sauce: It has lots of salt and umami flavor. Some recipes include this in place of salt; a little goes a long way.

Fresh herbs: Basil, dill, parsley, rosemary, sage, thyme, etc.

Fresh produce: Asparagus, cherry tomatoes, celery, oranges, lemons, limes, zucchini, berries, spinach, fresh ginger, and more—we always have a big variety.

Good-quality maple syrup: This is one of the few sweeteners I use. I love maple syrup because it's natural and contains vitamins and minerals.

Good-quality mayonnaise: My life wouldn't be complete without mayo. I love the real stuff but also like vegan for the milder flavor, perfect for salad dressings.

Micro-greens: These are packed with nutrients and are the perfect go-to for garnish. I throw some on just about every meal.

Mustard: Stone-ground and Dijon

Raw creamy almond butter: Baking with almond butter creates moist, delicious treats and makes for a protein kick in smoothies.

DAIRY

This cookbook is *almost* dairy-free; the only cow's milk you'll find is grass-fed butter in a couple of recipes. My entire household is sensitive to casein, the protein found in cow's milk, and cheese has the highest concentrated amounts. We've found that we can all tolerate a little butter here and there (along with sour cream and a few other items not in this book). We eat goat's and sheep's milk cheeses and yogurt often, since they are easier on the digestive system, are just as creamy, and taste as good.

Butter: Preferably organic and grass-fed

Manchego cheese: I could never completely give up dairy simply because I love cheese way too much. Manchego is made from sheep's milk and can usually be tolerated by people with dairy sensitivities. The taste is similar to Parmesan.

Plain sheep's milk yogurt

PROTEINS

Protein serves as building blocks for bones, muscles, cartilage, skin, and blood, so we eat our fair share. We always make sure the quality is top notch. We also eat the deer and elk meat that my husband and his dad have hunted, which is about as organic as it comes!

Eggs: Organic eggs are a must for us.

Grass-fed beef: This beef contains more omega-3s, CLA (conjugated linoleic acid), vitamin E, beta-carotene, and micronutrients (potassium, iron, zinc, phosphorus) than conventional beef.

Organic poultry: Chicken, turkey, and duck. I always have bone-in chicken breasts and thighs on hand in the freezer; on the bone makes for a more flavorful meal.

Wild-caught fish: Seafood is a staple in my house; we eat it a couple of times a week. These days, unless wild-caught, fish are farm raised and feed off grain or corn (usually GMO), making them not as nutritious as fish that eat sea vegetables and other fish in the wild.

IN THE FREEZER

Ezekiel Sprouted Whole Grain Bread: We only eat bread once in a while for toast or a sandwich. Ezekiel or sourdough bread (good-quality sourdough bread is fermented, which is good for the gut) are the only breads we ever buy.

Frozen fruit: Berries, cherries, avocados, cauliflower, and frozen bananas. Once you make a smoothie with a frozen banana, an avocado, or cauliflower, you will never go back. They make smoothies creamy and cold without using any ice. Peel the bananas and avocados, then throw them in a resealable plastic bag in the freezer. They keep well for a month. Chop steamed cauliflower, then place pieces in a resealable plastic bag in the freezer for a month.

ON THE COUNTER

Fresh produce: Garlic, shallots, onions, avocados, bananas, and more

IN THE SPICE CABINET

Chinese five-spice powder

Garlic powder

Ground black pepper

Ground cumin

Ground turmeric

Onion powder

Paprika

Red-pepper flakes

Salt: You won't find any white salt in this book; it has been stripped of all its nutrients. Pink Himalayan salt and coarse Celtic sea salt are packed with energy-rich iron, vitamins, and minerals—actually making them *good* for you.

Smoked paprika

Vanilla bean powder: I use this instead of vanilla extract when the brown color won't affect the recipe. Vanilla powder isn't as processed and is more potent than vanilla extract.

Vanilla extract (pure)

IN THE CUPBOARD

Arrowroot powder: Used as a thickener, it's the easiest starch for the body to digest. It is also free of gluten and GMOs, and is a healthier alternative to cornstarch.

Flours: In keeping with the no-white theme, there is no white flour in this book. Again, it's been stripped of all nutrients and is heavily processed.

> *Almond flour*
> *Coconut flour*
> *Oat flour*
> *Quinoa flour*

SWEETS

Cacao nibs

Coconut sugar

Dark chocolate chips

Raw cacao powder: Not to be confused with cocoa, cacao is packed with tons of vitamins and minerals–such as magnesium, calcium, sulfur, zinc, iron, and B vitamins–and is an antioxidant.

Raw honey

NUTS AND SEEDS

Hemp seeds

Raw almonds

Raw cashews

Raw pistachios

Raw walnuts

Sesame seeds

PACKAGED AND CANNED

Brown rice noodles

Canned black beans

Canned cannellini beans

Canned chickpeas

Chicken stock

Coconut milk: I like two canned ones: Native Forest Simple and Native Forest Classic full-fat coconut milk.

Quinoa

Quinoa flakes

Rolled oats

CONDIMENTS AND SAUCES

Tamari

Tomato paste

Worcestershire sauce

OILS

Coconut oil

Olive oil

Sesame oil

Toasted sesame oil

VINEGARS

Brown rice vinegar

Champagne vinegar

Red wine vinegar

White wine vinegar

HEALTHY EXTRAS

Chia seeds: This unprocessed, concentrated food contains omega-3 fatty acids, protein, fiber, antioxidants, and calcium.

Great Lakes Gelatin: One of my personal favorite products for multiple reasons: Gelatin promotes good gut health and skin health, protects joints, maintains strong bones–and the list goes on and on. We use it in multiple recipes as a thickening agent for treats like pudding pops and gummies. Not all brands are created equal, and if you use a different brand, you might have to play around with the ratio. Typically more generic brands are stronger so you won't need as much.

Maca: A vegetable grown in central Peru, it's rich in vitamins and minerals.

Matcha powder: This is a specially grown and processed green tea.

Spirulina: A natural algae powder high in protein, B vitamins, iron, and calcium, it's the most nutrient-dense food on the planet.

TOOLS

Food processor

Mandoline

Microplane grater

Nut-bag: Used for making nut milks, they are washable and reusable. Can be ordered on Amazon if your local home-goods store doesn't carry them.

Vitamix

BUT FIRST...

WARM COCONUT OATS

SERVES: 2 // **COOK TIME:** 15 minutes

I find oatmeal to be incredibly comforting in the morning. This recipe takes your ordinary oatmeal up a notch with thickening coconut milk and butter, plus hints of vanilla and cinnamon. Soak the steel-cut oats in water (to cover) overnight if you can, as this helps to soften them slightly before cooking, but if you can't, it's not a deal breaker.

1 cup steel-cut oats, soaked for 8 hours

1 can (13.5 ounces) full-fat coconut milk

¼ teaspoon vanilla bean powder (or extract)

¼ teaspoon pink Himalayan salt

¼ teaspoon ground cinnamon

1 tablespoon raw coconut butter

1 tablespoon pure maple syrup

1   Drain and rinse the oats.

2   In a medium pot, bring the oats and coconut milk to a boil. Reduce the heat to low and simmer for 15 minutes, stirring occasionally.

3   Remove from the heat and stir in the vanilla, salt, cinnamon, coconut butter, and maple syrup until combined. Serve immediately as is or with whatever toppings you like: ground flaxseeds, more maple syrup, shredded coconut, milk, or fruit.

BAKED OATMEAL
WITH WARM BERRY SAUCE

SERVES: 4 // **COOK TIME:** 15 minutes

Everyone in my house loves oatmeal. It's comforting no matter what time of year, is easy, and is versatile as you can throw just about anything on it. This version is quick, savory and sweet, and changes up typical oatmeal. I like using one berry for the oatmeal and a different berry for the sauce, for more depth of flavor and variety.

1 tablespoon coconut oil

½ cup raspberries, blackberries, blueberries, or strawberries

1 cup plain Almond Milk (page 216) or Cashew Milk (page 217)

1 cup rolled oats

1 egg

2 teaspoons pure vanilla extract

3 tablespoons pure maple syrup

1 teaspoon ground flaxseeds

Warm Berry Sauce (page 5)

1   Preheat the oven to 350°F.

2   Melt the coconut oil in a medium ovenproof pan over medium heat. Add the berries and cook for 2 minutes. Add the milk, oats, egg, vanilla, and maple syrup and stir to combine. Cook for another 2 minutes.

3   Place the pan in the oven and bake for 10 to 12 minutes. Sprinkle the flaxseeds and spoon the berry sauce over top to serve.

WARM BERRY SAUCE

MAKES: just over ½ cup

I will never forget a warm raspberry sauce I had over vanilla ice cream when I was in high school. For years and years, I tried to find something similar, and then once I started cooking, I wanted to make my own. This is delicately sweet and can be eaten on just about anything: ice cream, oatmeal, yogurt, pancakes, chocolate cake (or any kind of cake, for that matter), cheese—the list goes on and on.

---

1 tablespoon arrowroot powder

1 teaspoon fresh lemon juice

½ cup blueberries, blackberries, raspberries, or strawberries (if using strawberries, chop them)

3 tablespoons pure maple syrup

1   In a small bowl, dissolve the arrowroot powder with 1 tablespoon water and whisk to combine.

2   In a small saucepan, bring the lemon juice, berries, maple syrup, and 3 tablespoons water to a boil. Reduce to a simmer and cook for 4 minutes. Add the arrowroot mixture and cook for 5 minutes, until the mixture thickens substantially. Best used right away or keeps well up to 5 days in fridge.

WHIPPED YOGURT PARFAIT WITH CARAMELIZED PEACHES AND GRANOLA

SERVES: 4 // **COOK TIME:** 15 minutes

Nothing screams summer quite like ripe, juicy peaches. These creamy bowls of heaven are so good I could eat them every morning. Or afternoon. Or any time of day, for that matter! If you don't have peaches, you could use pears or even raspberries. Make this the night before so all you have to do is top it with granola in the morning.

3 cups plain sheep's milk yogurt

¼ cup pure maple syrup

1 teaspoon coconut oil

4 peaches, peeled and roughly chopped

½ tablespoon ground cinnamon

1 teaspoon pure vanilla extract

¼–½ cup granola (depending on preference)

1 With an electric mixer on high speed, mix the yogurt while slowly incorporating the maple syrup for 1 minute, or until fluffy.

2 In a sauté pan, warm the coconut oil over high heat. Add the peaches and cook for 10 minutes. Add the cinnamon and vanilla and cook for another 5 minutes, adding 2 tablespoons water if needed. Pour the mixture into a medium bowl and place in the refrigerator for 10 to 15 minutes, to cool slightly.

3 To build your parfaits, evenly distribute the yogurt among 4 mason jars or bowls. Top each with peaches and granola right before eating.

CHIA PARFAIT 3 WAYS

SERVES: 1 // **TOTAL TIME:** 1 hour 15 minutes

Chia seeds are healthy, little powerhouses loaded with fiber, protein, and omega-3s—and when soaked, they expand and turn into thick, creamy bowls of amazingness. The options for these are endless, so play around and have fun. No matter what, though, I think the Coconut Key Lime Chia Parfait (page 9) will always be my fave.

CHOCOLATE CHIA PARFAIT

SERVES: 1

¼ cup chia seeds

¾ cup Cashew Milk (page 217)

¼ cup coconut water

1 tablespoon pure maple syrup

½ teaspoon vanilla bean powder

½ teaspoon coconut sugar

1 tablespoon raw cacao powder

½ cup chopped cherries, divided

¼ cup cacao nibs

2 tablespoons peanut butter (optional)

¼ cup shredded coconut (optional)

1 Place the chia seeds, cashew milk, coconut water, maple syrup, vanilla powder, coconut sugar, cacao powder, and ¼ cup of the cherries in a medium mason jar or other airtight container. Give it a good stir, cover, and place in the fridge for least 1 hour or up to overnight (for best results, give it another stir or shake after 1 hour).

2 When ready to eat, stir and place the remaining ¼ cup cherries and the cacao nibs on top. Add the peanut butter and shredded coconut (if using). Keeps well in the fridge for up to 2 days.

BASIC CHIA PARFAIT

¼ cup chia seeds

¾ cup Cashew Milk
(page 217)

¼ cup coconut water

1 tablespoon pure maple
syrup

½ teaspoon vanilla bean
powder

½ teaspoon coconut
sugar

½ cup chopped
strawberries, divided

½ cup blackberries,
divided

1   Place the chia seeds, cashew milk, coconut water, maple syrup, vanilla powder, coconut sugar, ¼ cup of the strawberries, and ¼ cup of the blackberries in a medium mason jar or other airtight container. Give it a good stir, cover, and place in the fridge for least 1 hour or up to overnight (for best results, give it another stir or shake after 1 hour).

2   When ready to eat, stir and place the remaining ¼ cup strawberries and ¼ cup blackberries on top. Keeps well in the fridge for up to 2 days.

COCONUT KEY LIME CHIA PARFAIT

SERVES: 1 // **COOK TIME:** 10 minutes

1½ cups canned full-fat
coconut milk

1 tablespoon +
1 teaspoon lime zest

¼ cup chia seeds

1 tablespoon pure maple
syrup

½ teaspoon coconut sugar

1 teaspoon lime juice

¼ cup shredded coconut
(optional)

1   In a small saucepot, bring the coconut milk and 1 tablespoon lime zest to a boil. Reduce the heat to low and simmer for 10 minutes, stirring occasionally.

2   Meanwhile, place the chia seeds, maple syrup, coconut sugar, lime juice, and 1 teaspoon lime zest in a medium mason jar or other airtight container. Add the lime and coconut milk to the jar. Give it a good stir, cover, and place in the fridge for least 1 hour or up to overnight (for best results, give it another stir or shake after 1 hour).

3   When ready to eat, stir and sprinkle the shredded coconut (if using) or your favorite toppings on top. Keeps well in the fridge for up to 2 days.

ACORN SQUASH BOATS

SERVES: 4 // **COOK TIME:** 40 minutes

Whenever we have family or friends spend the night, I'll make these in the morning (okay, complete disclosure: Jay usually makes them), and we've never had one person not comment on how good and different they are. They're the perfect balance between salty (sausage), sweet (squash), and deliciousness.

---

2 acorn squash, halved and seeds removed

½ pound Italian sausage, casein removed

Coarse sea salt

2 ribs celery, chopped

Coconut oil, for the pan (optional)

4 eggs (optional)

1 Preheat the oven to 400°F.

2 Bake the acorn squash, cut side down, for 30 to 35 minutes, or until soft.

3 Meanwhile, heat a medium skillet over medium-high heat. Sauté the sausage with a big pinch of sea salt, breaking up the sausage, for 6 to 8 minutes, or until golden brown. Add the celery and cook for 1 to 2 minutes, or until tender. Place the mixture in a medium bowl and let cool slightly.

4 If making the eggs, lightly grease a skillet with the coconut oil. Cook the eggs to your preference (I personally like over easy or sunny-side up with this recipe).

5 Once the squash are cooked, scoop out the flesh, being careful not to tear the skin, and place in the same bowl as the sausage. Stir to combine.

6 Reduce the oven temperature to 350°F. Evenly distribute the squash mixture among the squash shells until almost full. Place a cooked egg (if using) on top of each squash and bake for 5 minutes. Serve right away.

SIMPLE BUT DAMN GOOD GRANOLA

MAKES: about 3 cups // **COOK TIME:** 10 minutes

Sweet and simple, eat this with yogurt, almond or cashew milk, or by itself for a light, healthy snack.

---

2 cups rolled oats

½ cup raw almonds, chopped

½ teaspoon ground cinnamon

⅓ cup raw honey

¼ cup hemp seeds

1 Preheat the oven to 375°F. Line a medium baking sheet with parchment paper.

2 In a large bowl, mix together the oats, almonds, cinnamon, honey, and hemp seeds. Press the mixture firmly into the lined baking sheet.

3 Bake for 10 minutes, or until golden brown. Let the granola sit for 20 minutes to harden before breaking it up. Store in an airtight container.

CARAMELIZED BANANAS

MAKES: about ¼ cup // **COOK TIME:** 15 minutes

I will always have a soft spot in my heart (or should I say stomach?!) for these simple, sweet caramelized bananas. This mouthwatering topping goes well on just about any breakfast dish—oatmeal, pancakes, toast, you name it—and is even delicate enough for dessert.

---

1 teaspoon coconut oil

2 ripe bananas, sliced

⅛ teaspoon ground cinnamon

¼ teaspoon pure vanilla extract

In a medium skillet, warm the oil over medium heat. Add the bananas and cook for 2 minutes. Add cinnamon and vanilla and cook for 10 to 12 minutes, or until the bananas reduce by about half. Serve over whatever you want!

DUTCH BABY

SERVES: 4 // **COOK TIME:** 25 minutes

I debated whether to put this recipe in the dessert section, since this pancake-meets-crepe can be eaten numerous ways. Eat it as is for a light, fluffy breakfast. Or have it for dessert simply with powdered sugar sprinkled over top, or folded up with chopped nuts and Caramelized Bananas (page 12) or peaches and topped with Warm Berry Sauce (page 5). The options are endless, and it always satisfies my carb craving (I've also increased the lemon zest to 1 teaspoon for a subtle lemon flavor—my current obsession). Seemingly elaborate, this can be thrown together quickly since most people have these ingredients on hand (buy arrowroot powder once and watch it last).

Coconut oil, for the pan

¾ cup plain Almond Milk (page 216)

1 tablespoon arrowroot powder

¾ cup oat flour

¼ teaspoon lemon zest

3 eggs

¼ teaspoon pink Himalayan salt

2 tablespoons pure maple syrup

2 teaspoons pure vanilla extract

1 Preheat the oven to 450°F.

2 Warm the coconut oil in a Dutch oven over medium-high heat. Once the oil is completely melted, turn the heat off and coat the pan, making sure to go up the sides as well. Set aside but keep warm.

3 In a high-powered blender, add the milk, arrowroot powder, oat flour, lemon zest, eggs, salt, maple syrup, and vanilla. Blend on high until smooth and well combined.

4 Pour the batter into the prepared Dutch oven and bake for 20 to 25 minutes, or until it fluffs up substantially.

5 Let cool slightly before adding any toppings (if using) and cutting into slices.

LEEK AND ZUCCHINI QUICHE

SERVES: 6 // **COOK TIME:** 45 minutes

Give me a quiche and a latte and I'm a happy girl. This quiche is time-consuming for a weekday morning, so make it in stages if you want (or just save it for the weekends). I always make my crust and filling the day before; then in the morning, all I have to do is throw them together and bake in the oven.

CRUST

1¼ cups blanched almond flour

½ cup arrowroot powder

2 eggs

½ teaspoon pink Himalayan salt

1 tablespoon coconut oil, melted

2 tablespoons cold water

FILLING

1 teaspoon olive oil

1 large leek, chopped

2 sprigs thyme, chopped

10 eggs

1 zucchini, chopped

1 teaspoon pink Himalayan salt

1 *To make the crust:* In a large bowl, mix the flour, arrowroot powder, eggs, salt, coconut oil, and water together. Place the dough on a floured surface and form into a ball (dough will be sticky). Wrap in plastic wrap and chill in the fridge for at least 1 hour or up to overnight.

2 Lightly grease a 9" pie pan and cover the bottom with parchment paper. Press the dough into pan, until the dough is about ⅛" thick (dough will still be sticky). Chill in the fridge for at least 30 minutes or up to overnight.

3 Preheat the oven to 350°F. Bake the crust for 5 minutes.

4 *To make the filling:* In a medium skillet, heat the oil over medium-high heat. Sauté the leeks and thyme for 5 minutes, or until golden brown. Remove from the heat.

5 In a large bowl, whisk together the eggs, zucchini, salt, and leek mixture until well combined. Pour over the partially baked crust and bake for 40 minutes, or until the center is set. Let cool about 10 minutes before serving.

ZUCCHINI BREAD FRENCH TOAST

The original plan was to just include my recipe for zucchini bread. But when I was recipe testing, I overcooked my loaf by about 10 minutes and luckily remembered that overcooked, or slightly stale, bread is perfect for French toast. So—voila!—French toast it is. My family specifically requests this for a weekend breakfast. I always make the zucchini bread in the middle of the week and let the loaf sit on my counter for a few days. This recipe makes an additional eight muffins, which hold the kids over until the weekend rolls around.

ZUCCHINI BREAD

MAKES: 1 loaf and 8 muffins // **COOK TIME:** 50 minutes

Coconut oil, for the pan

2 cups grated zucchini (about 1½ medium)

3 cups oat flour

1 teaspoon pink Himalayan salt

1 teaspoon baking soda

3 teaspoons ground cinnamon

2 cups pure maple syrup

3 eggs

3 teaspoons pure vanilla extract

1 Preheat the oven to 350°F. Grease a loaf pan and muffin pan with the coconut oil.

2 Place the grated zucchini in a paper towel or dishrag. Over the sink or a garbage can, squeeze out the extra moisture.

3 In a large bowl, mix the flour, salt, baking soda, and cinnamon until well combined. In a separate large bowl, whisk together the maple syrup, eggs, and vanilla. Add the zucchini to the egg mixture and stir to combine. Add the wet ingredients to the dry ingredients and mix well.

4 Pour just over half the batter into the loaf pan, so the pan is a little more than two-thirds full. Using the remaining batter, fill each muffin tin three-quarters full. Bake the loaf for 45 to 50 minutes, or until a toothpick comes out clean. Let cool 30 minutes. Bake the muffins for 20 to 25 minutes, or until a toothpick comes out clean. Let cool 15 minutes.

FRENCH TOAST

MAKES: 8 pieces // **COOK TIME:** 15 minutes

1 loaf zucchini bread (preferably 2–3 days old)

1 can (13.5 ounces) full-fat coconut milk, discarding the cream on top

4 eggs

1 teaspoon ground cinnamon

⅛ teaspoon ground nutmeg

Coconut oil, for the pan

1 Cut the loaf of zucchini bread into ½" slices, making 8 pieces of bread. In a large bowl, whisk together the coconut milk, eggs, cinnamon, and nutmeg until smooth.

2 Lightly grease a medium skillet with the coconut oil and warm over medium heat. Dip a slice of bread in the batter, making sure to coat both sides completely. Place the bread in the skillet and cook for 1 to 2 minutes on each side, until the egg is cooked and the bread is golden brown. Repeat with the remaining slices of bread.

3 Serve right away with chopped nuts, Caramelized Bananas (page 12), or whatever your favorite toppings are.

FLAX-BANANA-QUINOA MUFFINS

MAKES: 12 // **COOK TIME:** 15 minutes

Quinoa flour is great because it's gluten-free, light, and has relatively no flavor, allowing it to take on whatever taste you want—in this case, banana. Packed with tons of healthy omega-3s from flaxseeds, these muffins are a perfect snack to throw in your kid's lunch box, to have out when hosting playdates (as long as no one has a nut allergy), or for a light breakfast. My favorite way to eat these is warm with a little butter . . . mmm.

Coconut oil, for the pan

¾ cup quinoa flakes

¾ cup quinoa flour

¾ teaspoon pink Himalayan salt

1 teaspoon baking powder

1 teaspoon baking soda

1½ teaspoons ground cinnamon, divided

¼ cup + ½ teaspoon ground flaxseeds

2 very ripe bananas, mashed

½ cup pure maple syrup

½ cup plain Almond Milk (page 216)

3 eggs

½ teaspoon coconut sugar

1 Preheat the oven to 375°F. Grease a muffin pan with the coconut oil.

2 In a large bowl, mix together the quinoa flakes and flour, salt, baking powder, baking soda, 1 teaspoon of the cinnamon, and ¼ cup flaxseeds. In a medium bowl, whisk together the bananas, maple syrup, almond milk, and eggs. Add the banana mixture to the dry ingredients and stir until well combined.

3 Fill the muffin pan until three-quarters full. Bake for 8 minutes (they won't be done yet).

4 Meanwhile, in a small bowl, combine the coconut sugar and the remaining ½ teaspoon cinnamon and ½ teaspoon flaxseeds. Sprinkle over each muffin after they've baked for 8 minutes. Place the muffins back in the oven and bake for 4 to 7 minutes, or until a toothpick comes out clean. Let cool 10 minutes.

OATMEAL-ZUCCHINI MUFFIN CUPS

MAKES: 12 // **COOK TIME:** 20 minutes

Make these when you know you'll have busy mornings. They'll last for a week and are easy to grab and go. These are supposed to be breakfast muffins, so they aren't overly sweet, but if you want to add ¼ cup maple syrup, then go for it. I love these because hidden zucchini gives an extra greens boost.

Coconut oil, for the pan

3 cups rolled oats

½ cup plain Almond Milk (page 216)

¼ cup creamy almond butter

1 large zucchini, grated

4 ripe bananas, mashed

2 tablespoons hemp seeds

1 tablespoon baking powder

1 teaspoon pure vanilla extract

1½ teaspoons ground cinnamon

¼ teaspoon pink Himalayan salt

1 Preheat the oven to 350°F. Grease the muffin pan with the coconut oil.

2 In a large bowl, mix together the oats, almond milk and butter, zucchini, bananas, hemp seeds, baking powder, vanilla, cinnamon, and salt until well combined.

3 Fill the muffin pan until full or slightly overflowing. Bake for 20 minutes, or until a toothpick comes out clean. Let cool 10 minutes before transferring to a cooling rack to cool completely. Muffins will last up to a week in an airtight container.

BUTTERNUT SQUASH PANCAKES

SERVES: 4 // **COOK TIME:** 15 minutes

These are hands down the favorite pancakes at my house. Gluten-free, protein-rich, and fiber-filled, they are as good for you as they taste. And they're quick and easy to make in a pinch (I always make sure to have canned butternut squash puree on hand). You'll be hooked. Replace the butternut squash with pumpkin puree in the fall or sweet potato puree for a little variety.

4 ounces cooked butternut squash puree (just over ½ cup)

4 eggs

½ cup oat flour

½ teaspoon ground cinnamon

½ teaspoon baking soda

½ teaspoon vanilla bean powder

Pinch of pink Himalayan salt

Coconut oil, for the pan

1 In a large bowl, whisk together the squash, eggs, flour, cinnamon, baking soda, vanilla powder, and salt until fully combined.

2 Heat the coconut oil in a large skillet over medium-high heat until hot. Pour in about ¼ cup of the batter for each pancake. Cook for 2 to 3 minutes on the first side, or until bubbling, then flip and cook another 2 to 3 minutes, or until cooked through.

3 Serve immediately with butter and pure maple syrup, or your favorite toppings.

SWEET POTATO HASH

SERVES: 4 // **COOK TIME:** 30 minutes

This hash was all Jay. He truly enjoys making breakfast for the family, and I'll never complain about having a little break. He's been making this for years, and it's still one of our favorites because it's sophisticated enough for Father's Day brunch yet simple enough for every day.

2 tablespoons olive oil

1 small onion, chopped

1 large clove garlic, minced

1 large sweet potato, peeled and diced

½ pound breakfast sausage, casein removed

Pink Himalayan salt

2 eggs (optional)

1 large red apple, diced

1 cup roughly chopped packed kale, stems removed

1   In a large skillet, warm the oil over medium-high heat. Add the onion and garlic and sauté for 5 to 8 minutes, or until translucent. Add the sweet potato, sausage, and a big pinch of salt. Sauté for 30 seconds, breaking up the sausage. Reduce the heat to low, cover, and cook for 15 to 20 minutes, or until the sweet potatoes are tender.

2   Meanwhile, cook the eggs (if using) to personal preference (I like sunny-side up or over easy for this dish).

3   Add the apples and kale to the sweet potato mixture and cook for 2 to 3 minutes, or until kale has wilted, being careful not to burn the bottom of the pan. Remove from the heat.

4   To serve, place the eggs on top (if using).

LEMON-ALMOND-OAT PANCAKES

SERVES: 4 // **COOK TIME:** 15 minutes

Since we eat pancakes a few days a week, I like knowing they aren't loaded with empty carbs and ingredients that will weigh us down. These are made with almond and oat flours, which makes them gluten-free. Lemon brings a nice, subtle freshness (I'm obsessed with anything lemon these days), but feel free to leave the lemon zest and extract out and add ½ teaspoon ground cinnamon instead for a more traditional pancake.

1 cup almond flour

1 cup oat flour

1 cup plain Almond Milk (page 216)

2 tablespoons pure maple syrup

1 teaspoon baking powder

1 egg

1 teaspoon lemon zest

½ teaspoon pure vanilla extract

¼ teaspoon almond extract

¼ teaspoon lemon extract

Pinch pink Himalayan salt

Coconut oil, for the pan

1   In a large bowl, whisk together the almond and oat flours, milk, maple syrup, baking powder, egg, lemon zest, vanilla extract, almond extract, lemon extract, and salt until well combined.

2   Heat the coconut oil in a large skillet over medium heat until hot. Pour in about ¼ cup of the batter for each pancake. Cook for 2 to 3 minutes on the first side, or until bubbling, then flip and cook another 2 to 3 minutes, or until cooked through.

3   Serve immediately with your favorite pancake toppings.

EGG NESTS

MAKES: 12 // **COOK TIME:** 30 minutes

Chances are you've seen a recipe for egg muffins at some point. They were all over social media and every food magazine imaginable, and for good reason: their convenience and the endless possibilities for different combinations. This recipe takes them up a notch with a bottom layer of sweet potato that balances perfectly with the egg and pancetta.

1 medium sweet potato, peeled

1 tablespoon coconut oil, melted

⅛ teaspoon garlic powder

⅛ teaspoon smoked paprika

Pink Himalayan salt

12 eggs

½ cup cooked and chopped pancetta

1 serrano chile pepper, chopped (optional), be careful when handing

1 Preheat the oven to 375°F. Line a muffin pan with liners.

2 Using a cheese grater, grate the sweet potato into a paper towel or cloth. Squeeze out the moisture over a sink or garbage can. In a medium bowl, combine the sweet potato, oil, garlic powder, paprika, and a pinch of salt and mix thoroughly.

3 Evenly distribute the mixture in the muffin pan, until the bottoms are completely covered. Bake for 5 minutes.

4 Meanwhile, in a large bowl, beat the eggs and a pinch of salt. Pour on top of the cooked sweet potatoes, filling the pan about halfway up. Place a few pieces each of the pancetta and serrano peppers on top. Bake for 20 to 25 minutes, or until the eggs fluff up and center is set.

ASPARAGUS, PROSCIUTTO, AND ZUCCHINI FRITTATA

SERVES: 4 // **COOK TIME:** 20 minutes

Mornings are hectic with kids, no doubt about it. Rushing to get good food in their bellies before school can sometimes be a daunting task. Frittatas are great because you can throw whatever you want in them—and I love this particular frittata because it's full of veggies plus tons of protein from the prosciutto and eggs. And the real beauty of frittatas is that you can mix up the batter the night before (which is when I usually "make" breakfast anyway), and in the morning all you have to do is throw it in the oven. You could even bake it the night before so all you have to do is warm it up when you're ready to eat.

Coconut oil, for the pan

1 teaspoon olive oil

½ bunch asparagus, chopped (about ½ cup)

1 small zucchini, chopped (about ½ cup)

6 large eggs

⅓ cup chopped prosciutto

½ teaspoon pink Himalayan salt

1 Preheat the oven to 350°F. Coat a cast-iron skillet or other ovenproof pan with the coconut oil.

2 In a medium skillet, heat the olive oil over medium heat and lightly sauté the asparagus and zucchini for 4 minutes, or until lightly browned. Remove from the heat.

3 In a large bowl, beat the eggs until smooth. Add the vegetables, prosciutto, and salt and whisk to combine. Pour the mixture into the ovenproof pan and place on the stove over medium heat. Cook for 3 to 4 minutes, or until the edges start to cook, then place the pan in the oven. Bake for 10 to 12 minutes, or until the frittata rises and the center is set.

DUCK APPLE SAUSAGE

MAKES: 6 big patties // **COOK TIME:** 10 minutes

Duck is rich, creamy, and incredibly flavorful. My little Saylor goes nuts for these breakfast patties, always polishing off a few (the girl can eat!). Eat the patties by themselves, over a bed of greens, or with eggs and avocado for a full breakfast experience.

1 pound ground duck

½ red apple, finely chopped

½ cup chopped and packed spinach

1 teaspoon dried sage

1 teaspoon chopped fresh thyme

½ teaspoon ground black pepper

⅛ teaspoon pink Himalayan salt

Coconut oil, for the pan

1   In a large bowl, mix together the duck, apple, spinach, sage, thyme, pepper, and salt until thoroughly combined. Form into patties that are 2" in diameter.

2   In a large skillet, warm the coconut oil over medium heat. Cook the patties for 3 to 5 minutes on each side, or until completely cooked through.

THE LOADED EGG SANDWICH

MAKES: 2 // **TOTAL TIME:** 15 minutes

I'm obsessed with egg sandwiches for lazy, stay-in-your-pajamas weekend-kind-of-mornings. Their crave-worthy taste is good enough to be considered a cheat meal but, with the right ingredients, healthy enough not to be. Even if I eat two sandwiches, I'm still satisfied that I stayed within my healthy 80 percent.

2 pieces bread, such as Ezekiel sprouted bread, toasted

1–2 tablespoons mayonnaise

½ avocado, thinly sliced

2 thin slices heirloom tomato

2 slices prosciutto

2 eggs, cooked over easy or sunny-side up

Coarse sea salt

Ground black pepper

2 tablespoons micro-greens

Hot sauce (optional)

1 Place 1 piece of toast on a small plate. Spread ½ to 1 table-spoon of the mayo on top. In a thin layer, add half of the avocado on top of the mayo. Place 1 tomato slice on next, then 1 slice of prosciutto, followed by 1 egg. Season with salt and pepper. Sprinkle 1 tablespoon of the micro-greens on top and add hot sauce (if using).

2 Repeat on the other piece of toast.

SALADS

BRUSSELS SPROUTS AND AVOCADO SALAD
WITH CREAMY CAESAR DRESSING // 34

ROASTED TURKEY SALAD
WITH GREEN GODDESS DRESSING // 36

BBQ CHICKEN SALAD WITH PINEAPPLE
CHIPOTLE RANCH DRESSING // 39

BLT PASTA SALAD // 41

THAI BISON SKIRT STEAK SALAD // 42

SMOKED CHICKEN SALAD // 44

AVOCADO CHICKEN SALAD // 45

BUFFALO CHICKEN SALAD // 46

CHICKEN SALAD SWISS CHARD ROLLS // 47

SUMMER SALAD WITH
SWEET BASIL VINAIGRETTE // 50

BRUSSELS SPROUTS AND AVOCADO SALAD WITH CREAMY CAESAR DRESSING

SERVES: 2 // **TOTAL TIME:** 15 minutes

When I was pregnant with my second son, Jaxon, I lived on a Brussels sprouts and avocado salad from a Chicago restaurant. Here's my version, so creamy, thick, and satisfying you'll forget it's full of raw veggies and healthy fats.

2 avocados, diced, divided

1 small clove garlic, minced

½ cup plain sheep's milk yogurt

⅓ cup grated Manchego cheese

1 tablespoon champagne vinegar

½ lemon, juiced

2 teaspoons Dijon mustard

2 anchovies

Pinch of pink Himalayan salt

Pinch of ground black pepper

3 tablespoons olive oil

1 bunch Brussels sprouts, ends trimmed and shaved

1 Combine one-quarter of the avocado, the garlic, yogurt, cheese, vinegar, lemon juice, mustard, anchovies, salt, and pepper in a high-powered blender. Blend on high for 10 seconds, or until well combined. Turn to low and while the blender is running, slowly drizzle in the oil until smooth. You can drizzle cold water in, if needed, to adjust the consistency.

2 In a large bowl, mix the Brussels sprouts and the remaining avocado together until combined. Pour the dressing on top and toss to coat.

ROASTED TURKEY SALAD WITH GREEN GODDESS DRESSING

SERVES: 2 // **COOK TIME:** 15 minutes

Hands down, green goddess is my favorite salad dressing. It's rich and creamy, loaded with greens, and so yummy you wouldn't think it could be good for you. This recipe makes a big batch, but I tell my boys it's "green ranch," and they dip everything in it—from fish to veggies and chips—so we power through it quickly.

---

1 cup corn

1 large carrot, diced

2 teaspoons olive oil, divided

Pink Himalayan salt

2 cups sliced mushrooms

1 head Bibb lettuce, chopped

Green Goddess Dressing (page 37)

1 Maple Glazed Turkey tenderloin (page 55)

1 Preheat the oven to 400°F.

2 On a small sheet tray, place the corn and carrot with 1 teaspoon of the oil and a pinch of salt. Roast for 15 minutes, or until brown.

3 Meanwhile, heat the remaining 1 teaspoon oil in a small skillet over medium heat. Add the mushrooms and a pinch of salt and sauté 5 to 8 minutes, or until tender.

4 Place the lettuce in a large bowl. Toss with 2 to 3 tablespoons of the dressing. Add the turkey and vegetables. Divide between 2 plates. Serve with more dressing on the side, if desired.

GREEN GODDESS DRESSING

MAKES: about 2 cups

2 cups spinach

1 cup plain sheep's milk yogurt

1 ripe avocado, peeled and pit removed

2 cups basil

1 tablespoon fresh lemon juice

1 tablespoon white wine vinegar

½ cup olive oil

¾ teaspoon pink Himalayan salt

¼ teaspoon ground black pepper

In a blender, add the spinach, yogurt, avocado, basil, lemon juice, and vinegar and blend until smooth. Slowly drizzle in the oil until combined. Add the salt and pepper and blend to combine. Keeps well in the fridge for up to a week.

BBQ CHICKEN SALAD WITH PINEAPPLE CHIPOTLE RANCH DRESSING

SERVES: 2 // **COOK TIME:** 35 minutes

When I was in high school in Laguna Beach, I used to get Hawaiian pizza at least twice a week. Barbecue dressing on a pizza slice with pineapple and ham, dipped in ranch (not my healthiest choice!), was my absolute favorite. Here is a salad version so I can still satisfy my craving in a better-for-you way.

2 boneless, skinless chicken thighs

⅛ teaspoon garlic powder

⅛ teaspoon ground cumin

½ teaspoon chili powder

Pink Himalayan salt

2 tablespoons barbecue sauce (use your favorite)

1 romaine heart, chopped

2 cups mixed greens

¼ cup sliced scallions, divided

1 avocado, diced

½ cup sliced grape tomatoes

Pineapple Chipotle Ranch Dressing (page 40)

1   Preheat the oven to 350°F.

2   Season the chicken with the garlic powder, cumin, chili powder, and a couple pinches of salt. Bake for 30 to 35 minutes, or until the internal temperature reaches 165°F. Dice the chicken and coat with the barbecue sauce.

3   In a large bowl, add the romaine heart, mixed greens, 2 tablespoons of the scallions, the avocado, and tomatoes and toss to combine. Add the dressing to taste and toss again. Place the chicken and the remaining 2 tablespoons scallions on top.

RECIPE CONTINUES

PINEAPPLE CHIPOTLE RANCH DRESSING

MAKES: about 2 cups

1 teaspoon garlic powder

1½ teaspoons onion powder

1–2 chipotle chile peppers in adobo sauce, depending on how spicy you want it (be careful when handling)

1½ cups mayonnaise

1 tablespoon chopped parsley

¼ teaspoon ground black pepper

½ teaspoon dried dill

¼ cup plain Almond Milk (page 216)

1 tablespoon apple cider vinegar

1 round ⅛"-thick grilled pineapple slice, cored and minced

In a blender, add the garlic powder, onion powder, chile pepper, mayo, parsley, black pepper, dill, almond milk, and vinegar. Blend until combined. Remove and place in a small bowl. Stir in the pineapple until combined. Best to chill before serving.

BLT PASTA SALAD

SERVES: 4 // **COOK AND CHILL TIME:** 55 minutes

Always in heavy rotation at my house, this "salad" is easily my kids' favorite dish (it's up there on Jay's list, too . . . and mine). Creamy pasta with bacon—come on, there's nothing better. And it's even healthier with spinach substituting for lettuce. I've been known to make a double batch since the leftovers are even better the next day.

½ package brown rice macaroni

10 thick-cut bacon slices

2 cooked chicken breasts, diced

1 cup halved cherry tomatoes

3 cups roughly chopped spinach

1 cup mayonnaise

⅛ teaspoon garlic powder

1 teaspoon paprika

Pink Himalayan salt

Ground black pepper

1 Preheat the oven to 400°F. Line a baking sheet with foil.

2 Cook the pasta according to package directions and strain.

3 Meanwhile, place the bacon on the prepared baking sheet and bake for 6 minutes. Flip and bake the other side for 6 minutes, or until golden brown. Remove and roughly chop the bacon.

4 Place the pasta in a large bowl. Add the bacon, chicken, tomatoes, spinach, mayonnaise, garlic powder, and paprika. Season with salt and pepper and mix well. Chill in the refrigerator for 35 to 40 minutes, or until completely chilled.

THAI BISON SKIRT STEAK SALAD

SERVES: 2 // **COOK TIME:** 5 minutes

Light and fresh, this salad is perfect for a warm summer day. Simple in the best possible way, this salad leaves its mark with the delicious sweet orange dressing. Bison is my current favorite protein for its amazing health benefits: It's lean and grass-fed and has tons of omega-3s and conjugated linoleic acid.

SALAD

1 tablespoon tamari

1 tablespoon toasted sesame seeds

1 tablespoon fresh lime juice

1 orange, zested

1 teaspoon chili flakes

1 pound bison skirt steak

½ head oak leaf lettuce, shredded

3 cups baby spinach

½ cup roughly chopped bamboo shoots

3 scallions, sliced, white parts only

1 orange, peeled and chopped

½ cup chopped toasted almonds

DRESSING

½ cup fresh orange juice

1 tablespoon chopped basil

1 tablespoon raw honey

1 teaspoon sesame seeds

1 teaspoon sliced scallions

¼ cup toasted sesame oil

1   *To make the salad:* In a shallow dish or resealable plastic bag, mix together the tamari, sesame seeds, lime juice, orange zest, and chili flakes. Add the skirt steak and marinate for at least 1 hour or up to overnight.

2   Warm a skillet pan over medium-high heat. When the pan is hot, add the steak and sear for 3 minutes on each side, or until cooked medium. Let the steak rest for 15 to 20 minutes before thinly slicing.

3   In a large bowl, add the lettuce, spinach, bamboo shoots, scallions, orange, and steak.

4   *To make the dressing:* In a medium bowl, combine the orange juice, basil, honey, sesame seeds, and scallions. Slowly whisk in the sesame oil.

5   Toss the salad with the dressing to taste. Garnish with the almonds.

SMOKED CHICKEN SALAD

SERVES: 4 // **COOK TIME:** 1 hour 30 minutes

Knowing Jay loves smoky flavor and Kristin loves a flavorful chicken salad for lunch, we came up with this recipe that combines both of their favorite flavors. Perfect for a light snack or a hearty lunch, this salad is versatile and can be eaten on its own, wrapped in lettuce cups, or on a sandwich. **—MIKE**

1 small whole chicken

⅓ cup chopped almonds

⅛ teaspoon ground cumin

⅛ teaspoon paprika

1 teaspoon coconut oil

1 clove garlic, minced

½ avocado, mashed

½ cup mayonnaise

½ cup chopped celery

¼ cup chopped parsley

1 teaspoon fresh lemon juice

Pink Himalayan salt

1 Grease a grill rack with coconut, add wood chips (your choice) that have been soaked, and preheat the grill. Smoke the chicken for 90 minutes, or until the internal temperature reaches 165°F. Remove the meat off the bones and place in a bowl.

2 Meanwhile, preheat the oven to 400°F.

3 In a small baking dish, mix the almonds, cumin, paprika, and oil until combined. Roast for 10 to 12 minutes, or until golden brown.

4 In a large bowl, mix together the garlic, avocado, mayo, celery, parsley, and lemon juice until well combined. Add the chicken and almond mixture and stir to combine. Season with salt. Chill in the fridge for at least 1 hour before serving.

AVOCADO CHICKEN SALAD

SERVES: 4 // **COOK TIME:** 25 minutes

This chicken salad is nice because, instead of using a ton of mayo, avocado helps to act as a binding agent so you get the healthy fat benefits. Use a rotisserie chicken to save time, making this quick and simple to prepare.

2 cloves garlic

½ lemon

1 teaspoon peppercorns

¼ red onion, roughly chopped

⅓ cup chopped dill + their stems

2 bone-in chicken breasts

½ cup mayonnaise

1 avocado, mashed

½ cup chopped celery

Pink Himalayan salt

Ground black pepper

1 In a large saucepan, bring 5 cups water to a boil. Add the garlic, lemon, peppercorns, onion, a couple dill stems, and chicken breasts. Cover and simmer for 25 minutes, or until the chicken is completely cooked through. Remove the meat off the bone using two forks.

2 In a medium bowl, combine the mayonnaise, avocado, celery, chopped dill, and shredded chicken. Season with salt and pepper and mix until well combined.

3 It's best to chill this for 30 minutes, but it can be eaten right away. Serve as is or in lettuce cups.

BUFFALO CHICKEN SALAD

SERVES: 4 // **TOTAL TIME:** 1 hour 20 minutes

Buffalo sauce is my jam. I could put it on just about anything. When I'm in the mood for some spice and the perfect kick, this chicken salad is my favorite. Put it in lettuce wraps and serve with Carrot-Cashew Slaw (page 100), or eat it by itself with a spoon (my favorite way).

¼ cup mayonnaise

¼ cup + 2 tablespoons buffalo sauce or hot sauce

3 tablespoons chopped dill

½ cup chopped celery

⅓ cup chopped carrots

⅓ cup plain sheep's milk yogurt

1 medium shallot, finely chopped

1 teaspoon lemon juice

2 large cooked chicken breasts, diced or shredded

Pink Himalayan salt

1   In a medium bowl, combine the mayonnaise, sauce, dill, celery, carrots, yogurt, shallot, and lemon juice. Mix until well combined. Add the chicken and fold until evenly distributed. Season with the salt.

2   Chill in the refrigerator for at least 1 hour or up to overnight.

CHICKEN SALAD SWISS CHARD ROLLS

SERVES: 4 // **COOK TIME:** 1 minute

All of the chicken salads are good enough to eat alone, but if you want an added green, or just something to take outside without utensils, these rolls are perfect.

4 large Swiss chard leaves

2 cups Smoked Chicken Salad (page 44), Avocado Chicken Salad (page 45), or Buffalo Chicken Salad (page 46)

1 Cut the stems off the Swiss chard, leaving the leaves whole. Bring a large pot of salted water to a boil. Blanch the chard for 15 to 20 seconds, until bright green. Remove from the pot and cool in an ice bath to stop the cooking. Remove from the ice bath and pat dry.

2 Place ¼ cup of the chicken salad on half of 1 Swiss chard leaf and roll tightly. Repeat with the remaining leaves. Cut in half and serve.

SUMMER SALAD WITH SWEET BASIL VINAIGRETTE

SERVES: 2 // **COOK TIME:** 25 minutes

There's just something about roasted veggies and marinated tomatoes—they elevate this otherwise simple salad with depth and flavor. I love this salad when I've been going above and beyond my "cheating" 20 percent. It gets me back on track and reset, since it's light, fresh, and loaded with veggies. Make a double batch to eat the next day (just hold off on dressing it until you're ready to eat) and throw some cooked chicken on top if you want protein.

1 tablespoon raw honey

½ cup balsamic vinegar

1 cup halved cherry tomatoes

½ medium zucchini, diced

2 medium carrots, peeled and diced

½ eggplant, diced

½ tablespoon paprika

1 teaspoon garlic powder

2 tablespoons olive oil, divided

Pink Himalayan salt

Ground black pepper

½ cup corn

¼ cup chopped red onions

1 head red oak leaf or Bibb lettuce, chopped

½ avocado, diced

Sweet Basil Vinaigrette Dressing (page 51)

1   Preheat the oven to 400°F.

2   In a small bowl, whisk together the honey and vinegar. Add the tomatoes and let sit for 20 minutes to marinate. Drain and set aside.

3   On a large baking sheet, place the zucchini, carrots, and eggplant. Season with the paprika, garlic powder, 1 tablespoon of the oil, and a couple pinches each of salt and pepper. Toss to combine, then roast for 25 minutes, or until golden brown.

4 Meanwhile, in a medium skillet, warm the remaining 1 tablespoon oil over medium-high heat. Add the corn, onions, a large pinch of salt, and a couple pinches of pepper and sauté for 8 minutes, or until the onions are translucent.

5 Place the lettuce in a large bowl. Top with the roasted veggies, corn mixture, avocado, and marinated tomatoes. Pour the dressing on top. Divide the salad between 2 plates and serve immediately.

SWEET BASIL VINAIGRETTE DRESSING

MAKES: about 1½ cups

⅓ cup champagne vinegar

1 small shallot, minced

1 clove garlic, minced

2 tablespoons raw honey

4 tablespoons finely chopped fresh basil

1 teaspoon fresh lemon juice

2 teaspoons Dijon mustard

Pink Himalayan salt

Ground black pepper

¾ cup olive oil

1 In a medium bowl, whisk together the vinegar, shallot, garlic, honey, basil, lemon juice, mustard, and a pinch each of salt and pepper.

2 While continuously whisking, slowly drizzle in the oil until well combined. Season with salt and pepper. Keeps well in the fridge for up to 2 weeks.

BIRDS

ROASTED GARLIC AND
SAGE CHICKEN // **54**

MAPLE-GLAZED TURKEY // **55**

SUMMER GRILLED CHICKEN
WITH PEACH CHUTNEY // **56**

GRILLED BBQ QUAIL // **59**

CARAMELIZED
BLACKBERRY–GLAZED DUCK // **61**

MUSHROOM-STUFFED
CORNISH HENS // **62**

ROASTED GARLIC AND SAGE CHICKEN

SERVES: 4 // **COOK TIME:** 45 minutes

I debated naming this "Perfectly Baked Garlic and Sage Chicken" because this chicken truly is perfect. It's juicy and tender, and the notes of sage remind me of Thanksgiving turkey. This recipe has a ton of garlic since I'm a huge garlic lover, but feel free to cut it back if you'd like. Serve over a puree (page 118) with grilled veggies.

2 tablespoons olive oil

4 tablespoons chopped fresh sage

8 cloves garlic, minced

4 bone-in chicken breasts

Pink Himalayan salt

Ground black pepper

1 Preheat the oven to 425°F.

2 In a small bowl, mix the oil, sage, and garlic. Rub the chicken with the mixture, thoroughly coating it and making sure to get under the skin. Season with salt and pepper.

3 Place the chicken in a baking dish. Bake for 10 minutes, or until the skin starts to crisp. Reduce the heat to 375°F and bake for 30 to 35 minutes, or until the internal temperature reaches 165°F. Remove and slice to serve.

MAPLE-GLAZED TURKEY

SERVES: 4 // **COOK TIME:** 20 minutes

I pack my boys a lunch for school, and anytime I make them a sandwich with this turkey, they come home raving about how good their lunch was (otherwise it's crickets). This turkey is amazing by itself, thrown on a sandwich like the boys enjoy, and adds more depth to any salad.

2 turkey tenderloins

Pink Himalayan salt

Coconut oil, for the pan

1 teaspoon smoked paprika

3 tablespoons pure maple syrup

1 teaspoon chopped fresh thyme

1 Preheat the oven to 400°F.

2 Season the turkey with a few pinches of salt. Lightly grease a medium skillet with the coconut oil and heat over high heat. Sear the turkey for 2 minutes on each side, or until browned.

3 Place the turkey in a baking dish and coat with the paprika. Roast for 5 minutes, then remove from the oven and glaze with the maple syrup and thyme. Return it to the oven and finish roasting for 10 to 12 minutes, or until the internal temperature reaches 165°F and is completely cooked through.

4 Slice and serve however you want.

SUMMER GRILLED CHICKEN WITH PEACH CHUTNEY

SERVES: 4 // **COOK TIME:** 25 minutes

You know those nights when you're in a cooking rut and can't for the life of you think of ways to change up plain old chicken? Well, this is a true summer recipe utilizing ripe, juicy peaches during the months when it would be silly not to incorporate the gifts the warmer months have to offer. Keep the sides simple since the chutney is bold.

CHICKEN
4 bone-in chicken thighs

1 teaspoon minced curly parsley

1 lemon, zested

2 tablespoons olive oil

1 clove garlic, chopped

Pink Himalayan salt

Ground black pepper

CHUTNEY
Coconut oil, for the pan

1 shallot, minced

5 peaches, pitted and roughly chopped

6 chives, finely chopped

1 tablespoon raw honey

1 teaspoon smoked paprika

1½ tablespoons champagne vinegar (you can use lemon juice if you don't like the taste of vinegar)

1   *To make the chicken:* Place the chicken in a resealable plastic bag or baking dish. In a small bowl, combine the parsley, lemon zest, olive oil, and garlic. Pour on top of the chicken and coat evenly. Let marinate for at least 4 hours or up to overnight.

2   When ready to grill, season the chicken with salt and pepper. Coat a grill rack with cooking spray and preheat the grill to medium-high. Grill the chicken for 5 minutes on each side, or until the center is completely cooked through. Let cool 10 minutes before slicing.

3   *To make the chutney:* Meanwhile, coat a medium skillet with the coconut oil and warm over medium-high heat. To sweat the shallots, add the shallots to the pan and stir until coated with the oil. Cover and let cook for 5 minutes. Take the lid off, stir, then cover and cook for another 5 minutes. Repeat this process until the onions are soft and translucent.

4   Add the peaches and simmer for 5 minutes, stirring occasionally.

5   Add the chives, honey, paprika, and vinegar (or lemon juice). Stir to combine and let simmer for 5 minutes, or until slightly thickened. If the consistency becomes too thick, add a little water, about a tablespoon at a time. Season with salt and pepper.

6   To serve, spoon the chutney over the sliced chicken.

GRILLED BBQ QUAIL

SERVES: 4 // **COOK TIME:** 55 minutes

It's hard to get toddlers to try new things, but this is one of the clear-cut favorites of Kristin's kids. The small size of the quail, along with the dipping sauce, is perfect for young ones. It's also gourmet enough to serve to adults! Save the leftover sauce for the kids to continue dipping veggies and protein throughout the week. **–MIKE**

8 whole quail

1 teaspoon chopped thyme

1 tablespoon chopped parsley

¼ cup + 1 tablespoon olive oil

2 cloves garlic, minced, divided

½ teaspoon red-pepper flakes

1 teaspoon orange zest

Pink Himalayan salt

Ground black pepper

1 shallot, chopped

1 can (15 ounces) tomato puree

1 tablespoon tomato paste

¼ cup Worcestershire sauce

¼ cup balsamic vinegar

4 tablespoons pure maple syrup

½ teaspoon onion powder

2 tablespoons orange juice

1 Rinse the quail and remove the backbones with kitchen shears. Pat dry and set aside on a baking sheet.

2 In a small bowl, mix the thyme, parsley, ¼ cup olive oil, 1 garlic clove, the pepper flakes, and orange zest until combined. Rub over the quail and season with salt and pepper. Set aside.

3 Heat 1 tablespoon oil in a small saucepan over medium heat. Sweat the shallots by stirring them in the oil until coated, covering the pan, and cooking for 3 minutes. Add the remaining 1 clove garlic and cook, covered, for 1 minute, or until fragrant. Reduce the heat to low and add the tomato puree, tomato paste, Worcestershire sauce, balsamic vinegar, maple syrup, onion powder, and orange juice. Stir to combine. Simmer, stirring occasionally, for 20 to 25 minutes, or until the ingredients come together and the sauce thickens slightly.

4 Coat a grill rack with cooking spray and preheat the grill to medium-high. Grill the quail, occasionally turning and basting with the sauce, for 20 to 25 minutes, or until nice and charred or the internal temperature reaches 165°F. You can also broil the quail in the oven for about 15 minutes if you don't have access to a grill. Serve with sauce on the side.

CARAMELIZED BLACKBERRY-GLAZED DUCK

SERVES: 4 // **COOK TIME:** 35 minutes

I've been eating duck since I was about 10 years old. On Thursday nights, my mom would take my brother and me to a little restaurant by our house to get the duck special. Every time I eat duck, I think of that little café in Genesee, Colorado. This sauce is sweet and tangy, which pairs well with the rich heartiness of duck. Serve with grilled asparagus for a healthy, paleo-friendly meal.

Coconut oil, for the pan

4 skin-on duck breasts, patted dry

Pink Himalayan salt

¼ cup chopped red onion

1½ cups blackberries

3 tablespoons champagne vinegar

1 teaspoon Dijon mustard

2 teaspoons raw honey

1 teaspoon smoked paprika

¼ cup olive oil

1 Lightly grease a medium skillet with the coconut oil and warm over low heat. Lay the duck, skin side down, in the skillet and render out the fat for 25 minutes, or until the fat has decreased by half the amount. Place the duck on a cutting board and season with a big pinch of salt.

2 Preheat the oven to 375°F.

3 In a shallow pan, roast the duck, meat side down, for 8 minutes for medium-rare. Let rest for 10 minutes.

4 Meanwhile, in a medium skillet over medium-high heat, sauté the onion for 10 minutes, or until translucent. Add the blackberries and cook for 10 minutes.

5 Place the blackberries and onions in a blender and blend on high until smooth. Strain into a medium bowl. Add the vinegar, mustard, honey, paprika, and a pinch of salt and whisk to combine. Slowly drizzle in the olive oil while continuously whisking until combined. Season with salt.

6 Slice the duck and spoon glaze over top to serve.

MUSHROOM-STUFFED CORNISH HENS

SERVES: 4 // **COOK TIME:** 50 minutes

These are a mushroom lover's dream. The hens change up ordinary roasted chicken, and the mushrooms and herbs pack a ton of flavor. Elegant enough for date night, yet simple enough for a night at home in sweats and a ponytail—now that's my kind of meal!

4 whole Cornish hens, giblets removed

1 tablespoon coconut oil

½ cup chopped red onions

½ cup diced apples

2 cloves garlic, minced

6 cups assorted chopped mushrooms

1 tablespoon red wine vinegar

1 teaspoon chopped rosemary

½ teaspoon chopped thyme

1 tablespoon chopped parsley

1 tablespoon olive oil

1 teaspoon paprika

Pink Himalayan salt

Ground black pepper

1   Preheat the oven to 375°F. Rinse and pat dry the Cornish hens.

2   In a medium skillet over high heat, add the coconut oil, onions, apples, garlic, and mushrooms. Sauté for 8 to 10 minutes, or until the mushrooms reduce by almost half. Deglaze the mixture with the vinegar, stirring continuously. Remove from the heat and stir in the rosemary, thyme, and parsley. Cool until warm to the touch.

3   Stuff each bird equally with the mushroom mixture. Season the stuffed hens with the olive oil, paprika, salt, and pepper. Place on a large baking sheet, breast side up, and roast for 35 to 40 minutes, or until the internal temperature reaches 165°F.

FROM THE SEA

SMOKED WHITEFISH SALAD

SERVES: 4 // **TOTAL TIME:** 20 minutes

Until this recipe, I never went near "smoky" flavors. I left that for the men as the smokiness intimidated me. But after Mike made this smoked whitefish, I had to have the recipe, and I knew it would go into rotation at my house. It's perfect over a bed of lettuce for a light lunch or on sliced cucumbers as an appetizer for a party.

1 large fillet (16 ounces) smoked whitefish (or 2 smoked trout)

⅓ cup chopped celery

¼ cup chopped dill

1 tablespoon Dijon mustard

1 teaspoon lemon zest

1 tablespoon lemon juice

¼ cup mayonnaise

1 tablespoon minced shallots

1 teaspoon champagne vinegar

Pinch of pink Himalayan salt

1 tablespoon chopped pickles (optional)

1 tablespoon chopped parsley (optional)

1   Remove the fish meat from the skin and bones and break it into small pieces in a medium bowl. Add the celery and stir.

2   In a small bowl, whisk together the dill, mustard, lemon zest, lemon juice, mayonnaise, shallots, vinegar, salt, and pickles and parsley (if using). Pour the dressing over the fish and celery and gently combine.

3   Serve right away or, for best results, let chill for an hour.

TURMERIC-GLAZED MAHI MAHI

SERVES: 4 // **COOK TIME:** 10 minutes

I'm always looking for more ways to include turmeric in my diet because, with its powerful anti-inflammatory effects, it's arguably one of the best spices for you. The mahi mahi is a firmer, more flavorful white fish, and the bold hints of turmeric complement it perfectly, creating a savory dish.

4 fillets (6 ounces each) mahi mahi

1 tablespoon ground turmeric

1 tablespoon finely chopped chives

1 teaspoon smoked paprika

1 teaspoon lemon zest

¼ cup olive oil

Pink Himalayan salt

1 Preheat the broiler. Pat the fillets dry and place on a small baking sheet.

2 In a small bowl, mix the turmeric, chives, paprika, lemon zest, and oil until well combined. Reserve half of the marinade and liberally coat the fillets with the other half. Season with the salt.

3 Broil for 5 minutes. Pour the remaining marinade over the fillets and continue broiling on the same side for another 3 minutes, or until the fish is browned and slightly flaky.

SEARED SCALLOPS WITH BLACKENED CHERRY TOMATO AND SAUTÉED FENNEL

SERVES: 4 // **COOK TIME:** 20 minutes

This dish impresses easily without requiring much skill in the kitchen. Just make sure your scallops are completely dry so they sear instead of steam in the pan. And be careful not to overcook them—otherwise they become chewy. Open a bottle of white wine and sit outside to enjoy this perfect warm weather meal, if possible.

Olive oil, for the pan

12 large sea scallops

1 fennel bulb, thinly sliced

1 teaspoon fresh thyme

⅛ teaspoon garlic powder

1 cup cherry tomatoes, halved

Micro-greens for garnish (optional)

Coarse sea salt

1   Preheat the oven to 350°F.

2   Coat a medium skillet with olive oil and place over high heat. Once the pan is really hot, add the scallops and sear on one side for 2 minutes, or until browned. Flip and sear on the other side for 2 minutes.

3   Place the scallops in a medium baking dish and roast in the oven for 5 minutes, or until cooked through.

4   Meanwhile, in the same pan used for the scallops, sauté the fennel, thyme, and garlic powder over medium-high heat for 3 minutes, or until golden brown (add more olive oil if needed). Add the tomatoes and sauté for 5 minutes, or until charred. Remove from the heat.

5   Divide the scallops among 4 plates and top with the fennel mixture. Garnish with micro-greens (if using) and a pinch of salt.

SALMON SOBA NOODLE BOWL

SERVES: 4 // **COOK TIME:** 20 minutes

After discovering Kristin has a love for salmon and Asian food, I came up with this recipe, which is a no-brainer. I'm all about quick meals with great flavor, and that's what inspired this dish. Enjoy this year-round. **—MIKE**

---

1 pack buckwheat soba noodles

½ pound wild salmon

Pink Himalayan salt

2 teaspoons coconut oil, divided

1 tablespoon grated ginger, divided

2 tablespoons raw honey

⅓ cup tamari

¼ teaspoon fish sauce

4 tablespoons toasted sesame oil

2 teaspoons black sesame seeds + extra for garnish

1 tablespoon lime juice

1 teaspoon lime zest

⅛ teaspoon chili flakes

2 cups snap peas

2 bunches baby bok choy, chopped

½ teaspoon chopped garlic

1 avocado, diced

1 tablespoon chopped chives

1 Preheat the oven to 400°F.

2 Bring a medium pot of water to a boil. Cook the noodles for 3 to 5 minutes, or until tender. Drain and rinse with cold water until cool. Place the noodles in a large bowl and set aside.

3 Place the salmon in a small baking dish and season with a pinch of salt and 1 teaspoon of the coconut oil. Bake for 10 minutes, or until medium rare. Remove and let cool.

4 Meanwhile, in a medium bowl, whisk together ½ tablespoon of the ginger, the honey, tamari, fish sauce, sesame oil, sesame seeds, lime juice and zest, chili flakes, and 1 tablespoon water until well combined. Pour on the noodles to taste and toss to combine.

5 In a medium skillet, heat the remaining 1 teaspoon coconut oil. Add the snap peas, bok choy, garlic, the remaining ½ tablespoon ginger, and a pinch of salt and sauté for 5 minutes, or until the vegetables are tender. Place on top of the noodles, add the avocado, and toss to combine.

6 Evenly divide the noodles and veggies among 4 plates. Break the salmon into pieces and place on top of each. Garnish with the sesame seeds and chives.

BLACKENED HALIBUT

SERVES: 4 // **COOK TIME:** 15 minutes

A little spice and a lot of flavor—this halibut is a standout with a rich toasted cumin flavor. It's too spicy for my young kids, so I make this after they've gone to bed for an at-home date night or when girlfriends come over.

1 tablespoon paprika

1 teaspoon cayenne pepper

½ teaspoon chipotle powder

½ teaspoon ground cumin

½ teaspoon ground turmeric

1 teaspoon lemon pepper

1 teaspoon Aleppo pepper

1 teaspoon pink Himalayan salt

4 fillets (6 ounces each) halibut, skin removed

1 tablespoon coconut oil

1   Preheat the oven to 375°F.

2   In a small bowl, mix together the paprika, cayenne pepper, chipotle powder, cumin, turmeric, lemon pepper, Aleppo pepper, and salt until thoroughly combined. Liberally season both sides of the fillets.

3   Heat the oil in a medium skillet over high heat. Once the pan is hot, add the fillets and sear on each side for 1 to 2 minutes, or until slightly blackened. Place the fillets in a baking dish and bake for 8 minutes, or until the fish is opaque and flaky.

SPICY CRAB AND AVOCADO TOSTADAS

SERVES: 4 // **COOK TIME:** 10 minutes

This is a modern, healthy take on a traditional Mexican dish, bringing in crabmeat instead of ground beef, replacing refried beans with black beans, and baking the tortillas instead of frying them (just make sure to buy non-GMO tortillas). Skip the cheese and sour cream—you don't need it here as they're good enough on their own. I also leave out the cilantro since I'm not a fan of the flavor, but I know most people live for it, so I've included it in the recipe.

8 small corn tortillas

16 ounces cooked lump crabmeat

1 teaspoon lime zest

1 tablespoon lime juice

2 tablespoons mayonnaise

1 teaspoon paprika

⅛ teaspoon garlic powder

1 teaspoon chopped cilantro

½ teaspoon chili flakes

Pink Himalayan salt

1 can (15 ounces) black beans, rinsed and drained

1 teaspoon chili powder

1 large avocado

1 teaspoon ground cumin

½ cup Fire-Roasted Salsa (page 230)

1 cup shredded lettuce

Few fresh cilantro leaves (optional)

1 Preheat the oven to 350°F.

2 Place the tortillas on a large baking sheet and bake for 10 minutes, or until crispy. Let cool.

3 Meanwhile, in a large bowl, mix together the crabmeat, lime zest and juice, mayo, paprika, garlic powder, chopped cilantro, chili flakes, and a pinch of salt until combined. Refrigerate until ready to build the tostada.

4 In a blender, place the black beans, chili powder, 2 tablespoons water, and a pinch of salt. Blend until it reaches a smooth, saucelike consistency.

5 In a medium bowl, mash the avocado with the cumin and ⅛ teaspoon salt.

6 To build the tostadas, spread the black bean mixture in a thin layer on the tortillas. Spoon the crabmeat mixture on top, followed by the avocado and salsa. Garnish with shredded lettuce and cilantro leaves (if using).

SHRIMP AND SCALLOP LINGUINE WITH VEGGIES

SERVES: 4 // **COOK TIME:** 25 minutes

This dish will always have a special place in my heart because it was the first thing I ever made completely on my own. We had just bought our house in Nashville, and I was still getting used to the new kitchen. I had a few (okay, I had *many*) fails in the kitchen (homemade ravioli was the second thing I ever made—WTF was I thinking?!), and this was the recipe that gave me the confidence to keep cooking, because it came out exactly how I envisioned and tasted amazing with not a lot of effort.

½ package brown rice linguine

1 bunch asparagus, ends trimmed

6 tablespoons + 1 teaspoon olive oil

8 scallops, washed and patted dry

2 tablespoons minced garlic, divided

12 large shrimp, peeled

2 tablespoons white wine

1 cup halved cherry tomatoes

2 cups chopped cremini mushrooms

1 cup roughly chopped basil

1½ teaspoons pink Himalayan salt

¼ teaspoon ground black pepper

1 cup grated Manchego cheese

1   Preheat the broiler. Bring a large pot of water to a boil.

2   Cook the linguine according to package directions. Drain, place in a large bowl, cover, and set aside.

3   Meanwhile, line the asparagus on a baking sheet and drizzle with 1 teaspoon of the oil. Broil for 8 minutes, or until tender-crisp. Chop and set aside.

4   In a large skillet, warm 2 tablespoons of the oil over medium heat. Make sure the scallops are dry. Once the pan is hot, cook the scallops for 2 minutes on one side, then flip and cook for another 2 to 3 minutes. Remove from the pan, cover, and set aside.

RECIPE CONTINUES

5 In the same pan, sauté the shrimp with 1 tablespoon of the garlic for 4 to 5 minutes, or until cooked through. Place the shrimp with the scallops and cover.

6 Add the wine to the same pan. Add the mushrooms and sauté for 3 to 4 minutes, or until tender, scraping the bottom of the pan, if needed. Remove from the heat.

7 Using tongs to avoid any excess oil or water, place the mushrooms, tomatoes, and asparagus in the same bowl as the linguine. Add the scallops and shrimp, cover, and set aside.

8 In a different medium skillet over medium heat, warm the remaining 4 tablespoons oil. Add the remaining 1 tablespoon garlic and sauté for 1 minute, constantly stirring so the garlic doesn't burn. Add the basil and sauté for 30 to 45 seconds, or until wilted. Pour the garlic-basil oil on top of the pasta and season with the salt and pepper. Stir well to combine.

9 Add the cheese and stir once more, just enough to disperse. Serve immediately.

PROSCIUTTO-WRAPPED WHOLE TROUT

SERVES: 4 // **COOK TIME:** 20 minutes

Don't let the thought of working with a whole fish discourage you from making this recipe. For the longest time, I never went near whole fish. I would see great-looking recipes but stayed away because they seemed daunting. Don't let that be the case! This fish is light but has delicious herbs and the perfect balance of salt from the prosciutto. You can eat the whole thing (yep, even the skin) except the head and tail. Yum.

---

4 whole trout, cleaned and pin bones removed

1 lemon, thinly sliced, divided

8 sprigs dill, divided

4 sprigs thyme, divided

Pink Himalayan salt

Ground black pepper

½ pound prosciutto, thinly sliced

Coconut oil, for the pan

1 Preheat the oven to 375°F.

2 Stuff 1 trout cavity with a couple of lemon slices, 2 sprigs dill, and 1 sprig thyme and season with salt and pepper. Repeat with the remaining trout. Excluding the head and tail, wrap the trout completely with prosciutto slices.

3 Coat a cast-iron skillet with the oil and heat over high heat. Sear the trout on each side for 1 minute on each side, just enough to seal the prosciutto. Place in a large baking dish and finish cooking in the oven for 15 minutes, or until the center of the eyes turns white.

BROILED LEMONGRASS-MARINATED SEA BASS

SERVES 4 // **COOK TIME:** 15 minutes

Typically found in Thai dishes, lemongrass brings a subtle citrus element to this buttery, falls-apart-in-your-mouth sea bass. Just make sure to brush off the lemongrass before broiling as it's too fibrous to eat.

1 stalk lemongrass, chopped

2 tablespoons chopped basil, divided

1 tablespoon minced shallots

1 tablespoon lemon zest

1 tablespoon lemon juice

½ Fresno chile pepper, seeds removed and chopped (be careful when handling)

¼ cup olive oil

4 fillets (6 ounces each) sea bass, skin removed

Pinch of pink Himalayan salt

1　In a small bowl, combine the lemongrass, 1 tablespoon of the basil, the shallots, lemon zest and juice, chile pepper, and oil. Place the fillets in a large resealable plastic bag or baking dish and coat with the marinade. Place in the fridge for at least 1 hour or up to overnight.

2　Preheat the broiler to high.

3　Remove the fish from the bag and place on a baking sheet. Gently brush off the lemongrass and season the fillets with salt and the remaining 1 tablespoon basil. Broil for 10 to 12 minutes, or until the fish is opaque and flaky.

RAW HONEY PLANKED SALMON

SERVES 4 // **COOK TIME:** 20 minutes

Honey and salmon are quite possibly my favorite combo, especially with a touch of Dijon mustard . . . oh, baby! With tons of omega-3s and vitamins, wild-caught salmon is a superfood. I like mine raw in the middle, cooked medium rare, but feel free to cook yours to your liking. Don't worry if you don't have a cedar plank lying around—you'll miss a subtle smoky hint, but the salmon will still be delicious.

¼ cup raw honey

¼ cup Dijon mustard

1 teaspoon fresh lemon juice

1 teaspoon lemon zest

⅛ teaspoon garlic powder

Pink Himalayan salt

Ground black pepper

1 pound salmon fillet, skin on

1 teaspoon chopped fresh dill (optional)

1 Soak a wood cedar plank for 2 hours or up to overnight. Warm the grill over medium-high heat, or preheat the oven to 350°F.

2 In a medium bowl, whisk together the honey, mustard, lemon juice and zest, garlic powder, 2 pinches of salt, and 1 pinch of black pepper until combined. Liberally coat the salmon with the mixture and place on the soaked plank.

3 Cook on the grill for 20 minutes, or in the oven for 15 minutes, or until the salmon is cooked medium. Garnish with the dill (if using).

LAND ROAMERS

BISON STRIP STEAK
AND VEGGIE KEBABS // 86

VEAL BRACIOLE WITH
CASHEW RICOTTA // 87

GRILLED VEAL CHOPS
WITH GREMOLATA // 88

GRILLED STUFFED PORK CHOPS
WITH APRICOT GLAZE // 90

MAPLE-MUSTARD LAMB CHOPS // 93

BRAISED KOREAN SHORT RIBS // 94

BEEF TENDERLOIN WITH
RED WINE DEMI SAUCE // 96

BISON STRIP STEAK AND VEGGIE KEBABS

SERVES: 4 // **COOK TIME:** 10 minutes

One of my favorite things about summer is grilled meat and veggies—it just isn't summer without kebabs. Bison is a favorite of mine because it's incredibly lean. Let this marinade be your new go-to. It's salty and sweet and is devoured every time I make it.

1 pound bison strip steak, cut into 1" cubes

4 tablespoons olive oil, divided

2 tablespoons Worcestershire sauce

2 teaspoons balsamic vinegar

2 teaspoons raw honey

2 tablespoons chopped oregano, divided

2 tablespoons chopped parsley, divided

1 clove garlic, chopped

Pink Himalayan salt

Ground black pepper

1 large red pepper, cut into 1" cubes

1 large zucchini, cut into 1" cubes

½ red onion, cut into large dice

8–10 baby bell mushrooms, halved

1 In a large resealable plastic bag, add the steak, 2 tablespoons of the oil, the Worcestershire sauce, vinegar, honey, 1 tablespoon of the oregano, 1 tablespoon of the parsley, the garlic, and a pinch each of salt and black pepper. Massage the marinade into the meat to coat, then refrigerate for 1 hour or up to overnight.

2 Preheat the grill to medium-high.

3 Place the red pepper, zucchini, onion, and mushrooms in a bowl and mix in the remaining 2 tablespoons oil, 1 tablespoon oregano, and 1 tablespoon parsley. Season with a pinch each of salt and black pepper.

4 To build kebabs, thread the meat and veggies onto separate skewers. Grill for 5 minutes on each side while basting both skewers periodically with steak marinade.

VEAL BRACIOLE WITH CASHEW RICOTTA

SERVES: 4 // **COOK TIME:** 1 hour

I can't even begin to describe how in love I am with this cashew ricotta. I've been known to eat the leftovers with a spoon. Healthy cow's milk alternatives are, for me, the best thing in the entire world. I love that we can have the flavor and creaminess without hurting our bodies. You could also use this ricotta for stuffed shells, lasagna, or whatever your little heart desires! Or just eat it with a spoon, like me.

½ cup raw cashews

1 egg yolk

½ cup grated Manchego cheese

½ cup fresh basil

1 clove garlic

¼ cup olive oil + more for the pan

1 teaspoon lemon zest

Pink Himalayan salt

7–8 small veal scaloppine

Ground black pepper

1 tablespoon dried oregano

2 cups marinara sauce

1   Place the cashews in a large bowl and cover completely with water. Let soak for at least 4 hours or up to overnight.

2   Preheat the oven to 350°F. Rinse and drain the cashews.

3   Place the cashews, egg yolk, cheese, basil, garlic, oil, lemon zest, a pinch of salt, and ½ cup water in a high-powered blender. Blend on high until the mixture reaches a smooth, pastelike consistency, adding more water if needed.

4   Lay the veal flat on a cutting board. Evenly spread the cashew ricotta mixture in a thin layer on the meat, then carefully roll into pinwheels and tie off with butcher twine. Season the outside with salt, pepper, and oregano.

5   Coat a medium skillet with oil and heat over high heat. Once the pan is hot, add the pinwheels and sear each side for 1 minute. Then place in a small baking dish and spoon the marinara over the pinwheels until completely covered (you can also place any extra cashew ricotta in between the pinwheels and/or over top). Bake, covered, for 1 hour. Remove and slice to serve.

GRILLED VEAL CHOPS WITH GREMOLATA

SERVES: 4 // **COOK TIME:** 10 minutes

My boys always get a kick out of eating chops—I think it's because they love eating the meat directly off the bone. This gremolata is light and fresh, perfect for drizzling over top or used as a dipping sauce. Serve with grilled or roasted veggies for a healthy, satisfying meal.

3 tablespoons olive oil + more for the pan or grill

4 bone-in veal chops

Coarse sea salt

Ground black pepper

1 lemon, zested

1 clove Roasted Garlic (page 223), finely chopped

1 tablespoon chopped fresh parsley

1 tablespoon chopped fresh basil

1 teaspoon chopped thyme

1   Coat a grill or skillet with olive oil and warm over medium-high heat. Season the veal with salt and pepper and cook on one side for 4 to 5 minutes. Flip and cook for another 4 to 5 minutes, until medium-rare. Remove from the heat.

2   Meanwhile, to make the gremolata, mix the lemon zest, garlic, parsley, basil, thyme, and oil in a small bowl until combined. Add salt to taste.

3   Slice the meat off the bone. Serve with the gremolata over top.

GRILLED STUFFED PORK CHOPS WITH APRICOT GLAZE

SERVES: 4 // **COOK TIME:** 45 minutes

We don't eat pork too often, so when we do, we like to go all out and indulge. This rich dish hits all your senses: sweet, savory, salty, and smoky, making it perfectly balanced. Keep sides simple—opt for a light salad or grilled veggies as these chops are heavy on their own (and I say that as a good thing).

PORK CHOPS

4 1"-thick bone-in pork chops

Pink Himalayan salt

Ground black pepper

1 tablespoon coconut oil

½ cup chopped ramps or scallions

½ white onion, diced

2 cups chopped porcini mushrooms

1 cup diced apples

2 cups baby spinach

1 tablespoon chopped rosemary

1 teaspoon chopped thyme

2 teaspoons chopped sage

2 cloves garlic, minced

1   *To make the pork chops:* Heat the grill to medium-high or preheat the oven to 375°F.

2   Slice a 1"-slit into the side of each pork chop, moving the paring knife around side to side to create a pocket for the stuffing. Season with salt and pepper and set aside in the fridge.

3   Warm the coconut oil in a large skillet over medium heat. Sauté the ramps, onion, mushrooms, apples, spinach, rosemary, thyme, sage, garlic, and a pinch of salt for 15 minutes, or until tender. Let cool until it's warm to the touch before stuffing the pork chops.

APRICOT GLAZE

4 apricots, pitted and peeled

1 tablespoon smoked paprika

2 tablespoons olive oil

1 tablespoon raw honey

1 teaspoon red wine vinegar

Pinch of pink Himalayan salt

4 *To make the apricot glaze:* Place the apricots, paprika, oil, honey, vinegar, and salt in a high-powered blender and blend until smooth. Pour into a small saucepan and simmer over medium heat for 15 minutes, or until it reduces slightly. Let cool slightly.

5 Gently stuff each pork chop, evenly distributing the stuffing. If using the grill, grill the chops for 8 minutes on each side while basting with the apricot glaze. If using the oven, warm a grill pan over medium heat. Sear the chops for 5 minutes on each side, then place in a baking dish and cover with three-quarters of the apricot glaze. Bake for 20 minutes, or until the internal temperature reaches 155°F. To serve, slice the meat off the bone and spoon the remaining glaze over top.

MAPLE-MUSTARD LAMB CHOPS

SERVES: 4 // **COOK TIME:** 40 minutes

These chops are a go-to of mine—they're simple to make yet taste divine. The smoked paprika brings in a rich, smoky flavor that creates culinary heaven with the sweet maple and tangy mustard. Perfect for a weekday meal since they don't require much work.

3 tablespoons Dijon mustard

2 tablespoons pure maple syrup

1 tablespoon chopped parsley

1 teaspoon smoked paprika

1 teaspoon minced garlic

Coconut oil, for the pan

2 frenched racks of lamb

1   Preheat the oven to 350°F. Line a large baking sheet with foil.

2   In a small bowl, mix the mustard, maple syrup, parsley, paprika, and garlic until combined.

3   Lightly grease a skillet with coconut oil and heat over medium-high heat. Once the pan is hot, sear the lamb for 4 minutes on each side. Coat the lamb with half of the maple-mustard marinade. Bake for 25 to 30 minutes, or until the internal temperature reaches 140°F.

4   Cut the lamb into chops and serve with extra maple-mustard marinade on top or on the side as a dipping sauce.

BRAISED KOREAN SHORT RIBS

SERVES: 4 // **COOK TIME:** 2 hours

This recipe is one of my favorites. Even people who don't love Asian cooking swear by these bold flavors. It's a perfect meal for any season since the ribs are flavorful without being overly rich. The ribs pair well with the G&G cocktail (page 185). Make sure to marinate your meat for 8 hours or up to overnight for maximum flavor. **–MIKE**

½ cup toasted sesame oil

1 cup tamari

1 tablespoon fish sauce

¼ cup chopped chives

2 tablespoons sesame seeds

2 cups lemon sparkling water

2 tablespoons lime juice

1 teaspoon lime zest

2 tablespoons grated ginger

1 tablespoon chopped garlic

1 tablespoon Chinese five-spice powder

1 tablespoon chili paste (or hot sauce)

10 long cut beef short ribs

1 In a large bowl, whisk together the oil, tamari, fish sauce, chives, sesame seeds, sparkling water, lime juice and zest, ginger, garlic, five-spice powder, and chili paste until combined.

2 Place the ribs in a baking dish. Pour the marinade over it and massage the meat to coat. Let marinate in the refrigerator for 8 hours or up to overnight.

3 Preheat the oven to 375°F.

4 Add water to the baking dish, if needed, so the marinade comes halfway up the side of the meat. Cover with foil and braise in the oven for 2 hours, or until fork-tender.

BEEF TENDERLOIN WITH RED WINE DEMI SAUCE

SERVES: 4 // **COOK TIME:** 1 hour 35 minutes

This classic dish has been made many times at my house. Lately I've been using elk tenderloin (the hubs likes to hunt), but since I can almost guarantee you won't find elk at your local grocery store, beef is just as good and what I originally made the recipe with. This was the first dish I ever cooked for a crowd, and it still goes down in history as one of the best meals I've ever made. (When friends ask for the recipe the next day, you know it was a hit.)

BEEF TENDERLOIN
1 teaspoon olive oil

1 pound beef tenderloin

Pink Himalayan salt

Ground black pepper

2 tablespoons butter

1 sprig thyme

1 clove garlic

1 sprig rosemary

1 *To make the beef tenderloin:* Preheat the oven to 375°F.

2 Heat the olive oil in a medium cast-iron or ovenproof skillet over high heat. Season the tenderloin with salt and pepper and place it in the hot skillet. Sear on one side for 5 minutes, then flip and add butter, thyme, garlic, and rosemary to the pan. Once the butter is melted and starts to brown, carefully spoon the butter-herb mixture over the meat a couple of times to incorporate the flavors.

3 Place the skillet with the tenderloin in the oven and cook for 15 minutes, or until the internal temperature reaches 135°F for medium rare. Remove and let rest for 20 minutes before slicing.

RED WINE SAUCE

1 teaspoon olive oil

⅓ cup finely chopped shallots

2 sprigs thyme

1 sprig rosemary

1 clove garlic, whole

1 tablespoon balsamic vinegar

1½ cups dry red wine

4 cups unsalted beef stock

2 tablespoons butter

2 teaspoons raw honey

Pink Himalayan salt

Ground black pepper

4 *To make the red wine sauce:* Heat the olive oil in a medium saucepan over medium-low heat. Add the shallots and stir them in the oil until coated. Add the thyme, rosemary, and garlic clove and cook, covered, for 3 to 5 minutes. Add the vinegar and wine and simmer for 20 to 25 minutes, or until the mixture reduces by about half. Add the beef stock and simmer for another 40 to 45 minutes, or until the mixture reduces by about half again.

5 Strain the sauce into a large bowl and whisk in the butter and honey until completely combined. Season with salt and pepper.

6 Spoon the sauce over the tenderloin to serve.

FROM THE GARDEN

CARROT-CASHEW SLAW

SERVES: 2 // **TOTAL TIME:** 5 hours 5 minutes

I love cashews—their creamy resemblance to dairy milk when soaked and blended makes them a nondairy eater's best friend. This slaw pairs well with the Braised Korean Short Ribs (page 94), the Prosciutto-Wrapped Whole Trout (page 79), or on top of the Thai Bison Skirt Steak Salad (page 42). Use it as a garnish or as a simple, yummy side dish.

½ cup cashews, soaked for 4 hours + extra chopped cashews (optional) for garnish

1 teaspoon lemon juice

½ teaspoon lemon zest

4 large carrots, peeled and grated

Pinch of pink Himalayan salt

1 tablespoon chopped basil

1 Drain and rinse the cashews. Place in a high-powered blender with ¹/₂ cup water. Add the lemon juice and zest and blend on high until smooth. Pour into a medium bowl.

2 Add the carrots to the bowl and mix. Add the salt and stir to combine. Let marinate for 1 hour in the fridge.

3 Remove from the fridge and stir in the basil. Garnish with extra chopped cashews, if desired.

ROASTED BABY ARTICHOKES WITH AIOLI

SERVES: 4 // **COOK TIME:** 35 minutes

I grew up eating artichokes. My parents would steam them and serve with melted butter as an appetizer before dinner. Now my kids love them just as much as I did (and still do). They're the perfect hold-me-over until dinner to nibble on: light, fresh, and fun. The key to these is cleaning the artichokes correctly—don't be afraid to really get in there and peel those outer leaves.

9 baby artichokes

1 lemon, juiced

¼ cup olive oil

2 tablespoons red wine vinegar

2 teaspoons coarse sea salt

¼ teaspoon ground black pepper

2 cloves garlic, minced

1 tablespoon lemon zest

1 tablespoon chopped parsley

Aioli of choice (pages 233–235)

1   Preheat the oven to 425°F. Bring a large pot of salted water to a boil.

2   Clean the artichokes by peeling away the tough outer leaves until you reach the yellow-green leaves. Trim both ends and use a vegetable peeler to peel off the outer layer of the stem.

3   Add the lemon juice to the boiling water, then reduce the heat to a simmer. Add the artichokes and poach for 15 minutes. Remove and let dry.

4   In a large bowl, whisk together the oil, vinegar, salt, pepper, garlic, lemon zest, and parsley. Add the artichokes and toss to combine. Spread evenly on a baking sheet and roast for 18 to 20 minutes, or until golden brown and the edges begin to crisp.

5   Remove and serve with aioli on the side for a dipping sauce.

GARDEN CAULIFLOWER RICE

SERVES: 4 // **COOK TIME:** 20 minutes

Cauliflower rice has become quite the trend because it resembles rice almost perfectly but has many more health benefits. Cauliflower has a ton of vitamin C plus other vitamins and minerals. This "rice" is so good for you, consisting of basically just veggies and herbs, yet I always find it to be incredibly comforting.

1 head cauliflower, core removed and cut into 1" pieces

3 tablespoons olive oil

3 cloves Roasted Garlic (page 223), minced

1 tablespoon chopped shallots

1 medium eggplant, diced

1 small zucchini, diced

½ teaspoon ground turmeric

1½ teaspoons pink Himalayan salt

¼ cup basil, roughly chopped

½ cup cherry tomatoes, halved

1 teaspoon lime juice

½ teaspoon lime zest

1   Preheat the oven to 450°F.

2   Roast the cauliflower on a baking sheet for 10 minutes. Place in a food processor and pulse for 15 to 30 seconds, or until the consistency resembles rice. Set aside.

3   In a large skillet, warm the oil over medium-high heat. Add the garlic and shallots and sauté for 2 minutes, or until aromatic. Add the eggplant and zucchini and sauté 5 to 8 minutes, or until the eggplant is tender. Add the cauliflower to the skillet with the turmeric, salt, and basil. Stir to combine.

4   Remove from the heat and stir in the tomatoes and lime juice and zest. Serve warm.

WARM TRUMPET MUSHROOMS WITH POACHED EGGS AND TOASTED QUINOA

SERVES: 2 // **COOK TIME:** 30 minutes

While in LA a few years back, I had a dish similar to this at a sushi restaurant, and as soon as I got home, I started trying to re-create it. Toasted quinoa gives this dish just the right amount of crunch, and the runny poached eggs give depth to the warm mushrooms and spinach. Trumpet mushrooms are easily found at most well-stocked grocery stores (or farmers' markets), but if you don't have access to them, you could try chanterelle or cremini mushrooms instead.

¼ cup uncooked quinoa

1 teaspoon melted + ¼ cup (not melted) coconut oil

1 teaspoon smoked paprika

Pink Himalayan salt

5 scallions, chopped

1 tablespoon chopped shallots

1 clove garlic, minced

1 pound trumpet mushrooms, roughly chopped

1 tablespoon balsamic vinegar

1 teaspoon Worcestershire sauce

1 teaspoon chopped thyme

1 tablespoon chopped sage

1 tablespoon chopped rosemary

2 eggs

1 tablespoon white wine vinegar

1 cup spinach

½ teaspoon olive oil

1 small wedge lemon

1 tablespoon chopped parsley

1 Preheat the oven to 375°F.

2 In a baking dish, toss the quinoa with 1 teaspoon melted coconut oil, the paprika, and a big pinch of salt. Bake for 10 minutes, or until browned. Set aside.

3 Heat ¼ cup coconut oil in a large skillet over medium-high heat. Sauté the scallions, shallots, and garlic for 2 minutes. Add the mushrooms and sauté for 5 minutes. Add the balsamic vinegar and Worcestershire sauce and sauté for another 5 minutes. Remove from the heat and stir in the thyme, sage, and rosemary and season with salt to taste. Set aside.

4 Crack the eggs in 2 separate small bowls or ramekins. In a medium pot, simmer enough water so the eggs will be fully submerged with a pinch of salt and the white wine vinegar. With a spoon, start a stirring motion, or a whirlpool, in the water. Gently pour the eggs, one at a time, into the center of the pot. Let poach for 3 to 5 minutes. To remove, use a slotted spoon and place each egg on a paper towel.

5 Place the spinach in the bottom of a serving bowl. Add the olive oil and a squeeze of lemon. Toss to coat. Add the warm mushrooms over the greens, then place the poached eggs over mushrooms. Garnish with parsley and toasted quinoa. Serve immediately.

BUTTER-POACHED WHITE ASPARAGUS

SERVES: 4 // **COOK TIME:** 20 minutes

Sometimes I just need a little butter in my life (or in this case, an entire stick!). I believe in having balance and everything in moderation; therefore, I've used butter in a few recipes (this cookbook is how I truly eat, so I wasn't going to hold back). And I decided that asparagus is just better with some damn butter! Not only does it taste amazing, your house is going to smell delicious with the herb butter cooking on your stove.

---

1 stick butter

1 teaspoon chopped garlic

1 teaspoon lemon zest

1 tablespoon chopped dill

1 sprig thyme

1 small bay leaf

Pinch of pink Himalayan salt

1 bunch white asparagus, ends trimmed

In a skillet large enough to hold the asparagus in a single layer, melt the butter over low heat with the garlic, lemon zest, dill, thyme, bay leaf, and salt. Add the asparagus, cover, and poach for 20 minutes, or until a knife slides easily through the thick end of the asparagus.

APPLE-FENNEL SLAW

SERVES: 2 // **TOTAL TIME:** 15 minutes

I only recently started eating fennel (thanks to breastfeeding—it's known to support a healthy milk supply), and it's become a new favorite of mine. A simple preparation, this is perfect on top of pork or chicken. Fennel paired with apples makes for a more interesting side dish, one with tons of vitamins and minerals that are great for overall heart health.

2 medium red apples, thinly sliced and halved

2 small fennel bulbs, julienned

1 teaspoon lemon juice

Pink Himalayan salt

½ shallot, thinly sliced

1 tablespoon chopped parsley

1 tablespoon chopped fennel leaves

1 tablespoon coconut oil, melted

1 teaspoon white wine vinegar

1 teaspoon Calabrian chili flakes

Place the apples and fennel bulbs in a medium bowl. Add the lemon juice and a big pinch of salt and stir to combine. Stir in the shallot, parsley, fennel leaves, oil, vinegar, and chili flakes.

SUNCHOKE BRAVAS WITH FERMENTED CHILI SAUCE

SERVES: 4 // **COOK TIME:** 20 minutes

One crisp fall day, I called my local grocery store to see if they had sunchokes in stock (they are seasonal). After talking to three different people, no one could tell me because no one knew what they were. Well, my friends, you may not have heard of sunchokes until now, but chances are, you will remain a loyal customer from here on out. A healthy alternative to potatoes, sunchokes have a ton of fiber and are good for the digestive system. The first time I had these, I had no clue what I was eating, but now they are always in rotation at my house.

¼ cup gochujang paste

1 tablespoon white wine vinegar

1 teaspoon raw honey

1 teaspoon smoked paprika

½ teaspoon pink Himalayan salt + extra for seasoning

2 cups coconut oil

10 medium sunchokes, peeled and quartered

1 teaspoon paprika

1 teaspoon ground cumin

1 teaspoon Calabrian chili flakes

1   In a medium bowl, whisk together the gochujang paste, vinegar, honey, paprika, and ¼ cup water until well combined. Season with salt to taste. Let sit for 1 hour or up to overnight.

2   Heat the oil in a medium pot over medium-high heat. Fry the sunchokes for 15 to 18 minutes, or until golden brown and tender, stirring occasionally so they don't stick together. Remove and toss in a bowl with the paprika, cumin, chili flakes, and ½ teaspoon salt.

3   Serve with the chili sauce on the side or tossed on the sunchokes.

GREEN BEAN FRIES WITH YOGURT DILL DIP

SERVES: 4 // **COOK TIME:** 25 minutes

Green beans or not, say the word *fry* and my kids are in (especially with a dipping sauce). I'm always looking for ways to get more veggies in for my entire family, not just my kids. These "fries" are healthy since they're actually a veggie yet manage to satisfy the fry craving. Plus, this yogurt dill sauce is amazing and is good to dip many veggies in, such as broccoli or carrots, so it's good to have on hand. I use vegan mayo for the dip because I find it has a slightly blander taste—which I think is a good thing—but feel free to use regular mayo. Make the dip first, since it needs to sit in the fridge for at least 30 minutes.

2 tablespoons olive oil + extra for the baking sheets

1 pound fresh green beans, ends trimmed

2 large egg yolks

¼ cup almond flour

¼ cup grated Manchego cheese

1 teaspoon pink Himalayan salt

1 teaspoon garlic powder

1 teaspoon paprika

1 teaspoon ground black pepper

Yogurt Dill Dip (page 113)

1 Preheat the oven to 425°F. Line 2 baking sheets with parchment paper and drizzle with olive oil.

2 Place the green beans, egg yolks, and oil in a large bowl. Mix well with your hands until the green beans are completely coated. Add the almond flour, cheese, salt, garlic powder, paprika, and pepper and toss to coat.

3 Spread the green beans on the prepared baking sheets and bake for 20 to 25 minutes, or until crispy. Serve with the Yogurt Dill dip.

YOGURT DILL DIP

MAKES: about 2 cups

1 cup plain sheep's milk yogurt

½ cup vegan mayonnaise

¼ cup chopped dill

½ teaspoon garlic powder

1 tablespoon lemon juice

Pinch of pink Himalayan salt

Pinch of ground black pepper

In a small bowl, whisk together the yogurt, mayo, dill, garlic powder, lemon juice, salt, and pepper until well combined. Let sit in the refrigerator for at least 30 minutes or up to overnight.

SLAW WITH TAHINI DRESSING

SERVES: 4 // **TOTAL TIME:** 45 minutes

I love anything with an Asian flair. Made with brown rice vinegar, tahini, and tamari, this slaw has just that. My kids specifically ask for this and have been known to snack on leftovers.

1 cucumber, julienned

1 teaspoon pink Himalayan salt

1 large carrot, peeled and julienned

¼ small head cabbage, chopped (just over 1 cup)

3 green onions, white parts only, sliced

¼ cup brown rice vinegar

2 tablespoons tahini

1 teaspoon minced garlic

4 tablespoons tamari

1 tablespoon raw honey

1   Place the cucumber in a colander. Sprinkle with the salt and let stand for 15 minutes to release moisture. Rinse and drain.

2   Meanwhile, place the carrot, cabbage, and onions in a large bowl.

3   In a medium bowl, whisk together the vinegar, tahini, garlic, tamari, and honey until well combined.

4   Add the cucumbers to the veggies in the large bowl and pour the dressing over. Toss to coat. Let sit for 15 minutes for the flavors to combine.

ROASTED PARSLEY ROOT

SERVES: 4 // **COOK TIME:** 25 minutes

Poor parsley root doesn't get the love I think it deserves. I'm guessing you've never had it since most people don't think to go near it. Well, it's loaded with vitamins, is a strong antioxidant, and has a relatively mild flavor, allowing it to pair well with just about anything.

4 medium parsley roots (or 1 large celery root), peeled and cut into 1" cubes

¼ cup coconut oil, melted

1 tablespoon chopped oregano

1 tablespoon chopped parsley

⅛ teaspoon garlic powder

2 tablespoons white wine

Pinch of pink Himalayan salt

1 Preheat the oven to 400°F.

2 In a large bowl, toss the parsley roots with the oil, oregano, parsley, garlic powder, wine, and salt. Lay out the parsley roots on a large baking sheet with space between each piece. Roast for 20 to 25 minutes, or until fork-tender and golden brown.

RAW SHAVED ASPARAGUS SALAD

SERVES: 4 // **TOTAL TIME:** 50 minutes

Fresh and with only a few ingredients, this dish is pretty and colorful with green and purple asparagus. Purple is seasonal, so if you can't find it, then just use two bunches of greens—it will taste exactly the same. The key to this salad is cutting the asparagus and carrot super thin. I prefer using a peeler over a mandoline (I find it's also faster). I love this as a side with the Prosciutto-Wrapped Whole Trout (page 79).

1 bunch large green asparagus, ends trimmed

1 bunch large purple asparagus, ends trimmed

1 medium carrot, peeled

Pink Himalayan salt

2 tablespoons chopped basil

1 tablespoon lemon juice

1 tablespoon champagne vinegar

1 tablespoon raw honey

¼ cup olive oil

1   Using a vegetable peeler or mandoline, thinly shave the green and purple asparagus and the carrot into a large bowl. Mix in a couple of pinches of salt and let sit for 20 minutes. Drain off any excess liquid.

2   In a medium bowl, combine the basil, lemon juice, vinegar, and honey. Slowly whisk in the oil until combined. Add the dressing to the vegetables and toss to coat.

PUREES

There are only two things you need to make any dish look restaurant quality: micro-greens (for garnish) and a puree. Brush any puree on the bottom of a plate, put fish or meat on top, and garnish with micro-greens. Trust me, it will make every meal picture worthy. Ahead are three of my favorite purees, but once you get the hang of it, you can pretty much make whatever kind you want.

Use the Parsnip Puree with any red meat, specifically the Braised Korean Short Ribs (page 94) or the Caramelized Blackberry–Glazed Duck (page 61). The Golden Beet Puree is great under the Roasted Garlic and Sage Chicken (page 54) or Mushroom-Stuffed Cornish Hens (page 62). And the English Pea Puree goes well with the Seared Scallops (page 68) or any seafood.

PARSNIP (OR CELERY ROOT) PURÉE

MAKES: about 2 cups // **COOK TIME:** 35 minutes

3 parsnips (or 2 small celery roots), peeled and cubed

Olive oil

Pink Himalayan salt

2 cups chicken stock

1 clove Roasted Garlic (page 223)

1 Preheat the oven to 400°F.

2 Soak the parsnips in a large bowl of ice water for 5 minutes to remove the bitterness (skip this step if using celery root). Remove and pat dry.

3 Place the parsnips or celery roots on a large baking sheet. Coat with olive oil and a big pinch of salt. Roast for 20 to 25 minutes, or until golden brown.

4 Remove from the oven and place the parsnips or celery roots in a medium pot with the stock and garlic. Cook over medium heat for 10 minutes to bring the flavors together.

5 Place the parsnips or celery roots and 1 cup of the stock in a high-powered blender. Add 1 tablespoon olive oil and $1/2$ teaspoon salt and blend until smooth, adding more stock as needed if the consistency is too thick.

GOLDEN BEET PUREE

MAKES: about 2 cups // **COOK TIME:** 35 minutes

1 teaspoon coconut oil

½ sweet onion, sliced

4 cups chicken or
vegetable stock

1 clove garlic

1 bay leaf

1 pound golden beets,
peeled and cubed

⅓ cup plain sheep's milk
yogurt

½ teaspoon pink
Himalayan salt

1 Warm the oil in a medium skillet over medium heat. Sauté the onions for 12 minutes, or until caramelized.

2 Meanwhile, in a medium pot, bring the stock, garlic, and bay leaf to a boil. Add the beets and simmer for 30 to 35 minutes, or until fork-tender.

3 Remove the beets and garlic from the pot, reserving the stock, and place in a blender. Add the yogurt, salt, and onions and blend until smooth, adding stock if needed for desired consistency.

ENGLISH PEA PUREE

MAKES: about 2 cups // **COOK TIME:** 5 minutes

2 cups vegetable stock

2 cups frozen English
peas

1 tablespoon chopped
basil

1 teaspoon lemon zest

¼ cup soft goat cheese

Big pinch of pink
Himalayan salt

Ground black pepper

In a medium pot, bring the stock to a boil. Add the peas and simmer for 5 minutes. Reserving the stock, remove the peas and place in a blender. Add the basil, lemon zest, goat cheese, salt, and a pinch of pepper. Blend on high, adding stock a little at a time, until the mixture reaches smooth consistency.

SIDES AND SUCH

CREAMY CHICKPEAS AND SPINACH

SERVES: 4 // **TOTAL TIME:** 35 minutes

Yogurt, aioli, and chickpeas are a combo I never knew I needed. Together with the spinach, they create culinary bliss. If you don't have Roasted Garlic Aioli (page 234) on hand, use 2 tablespoons mayo and 1 minced clove of garlic. If you can, let this dish sit for a few hours so the flavors combine. I made this for lunch, then snacked on it after it sat for about 4 hours, and that was the best it's ever tasted. Also great with avocado and chicken as a main dish.

1 can cooked chickpeas, drained

4 cups spinach, roughly chopped

½ small shallot, thinly sliced

½ cup plain sheep's milk yogurt

2 tablespoon Roasted Garlic Aioli (page 234)

1 teaspoon lemon juice

½ teaspoon lemon zest

1 tablespoon chopped basil

⅛ teaspoon ground cumin

Pinch of pink Himalayan salt

1   Place the chickpeas and spinach in a medium bowl.

2   In a small bowl, whisk together the shallot, yogurt, aioli, lemon juice and zest, basil, cumin, and salt until well combined. Fold the mixture into the spinach and chickpeas. Let sit in the refrigerator for about 20 minutes or up to overnight, for the flavors to combine.

CARROT AND LEEK LENTILS

MAKES: about 3 cups // **COOK TIME:** 15 minutes

Warm, hearty, and comforting, this can be made for a vegan lunch or as a side. I find lentils make a very filling, satisfying dish without weighing me down.

---

2 tablespoons + ¼ cup extra virgin olive oil

1 leek, sliced in ¼" rounds

2 carrots, peeled and diced

1 teaspoon minced garlic

1 cup red lentils

4 teaspoons Dijon mustard

1½ teaspoons red wine vinegar

2 teaspoons pink Himalayan salt

¾ teaspoon ground black pepper

1   In a medium skillet, heat 2 tablespoons oil over medium heat. Sauté the leek and carrots for 5 minutes, or until slightly tender. Add the garlic and sauté 1 minute, then remove from the heat.

2   Rinse and drain the lentils. In a medium saucepan, add the lentils to 4 cups water and bring to a boil. Add the carrots and leeks and reduce heat, simmering for 8 minutes, or until the lentils are tender. Drain, then place the lentils, carrots, and leeks in a large bowl.

3   In a small bowl, whisk together ¼ cup oil, the mustard, vinegar, salt, and pepper. Pour over the lentils and stir to combine. Let cool for 15 minutes before serving.

BAKED WHITE BEANS

SERVES: 4 // **COOK TIME:** 35 minutes

Baked beans remind me of family BBQs growing up—I used to get excited whenever I saw them. They're easily my favorite side dish for their beautiful, mouthwatering flavor. Today, I make these in the summer for our own family BBQs or during the winter months for a warm, comforting side dish. Serve with beer chicken and grilled veggies for the perfect all-American summer meal.

5 slices bacon, chopped

1 cup minced white onions

4 cups canned navy beans

⅛ teaspoon garlic powder

1 teaspoon smoked paprika

2 tablespoons pure maple syrup

1 cup jarred tomato sauce

Pinch of pink Himalayan salt

Pinch of ground black pepper

1 In a large skillet over medium heat, sauté the bacon and onions for 8 to 10 minutes, or until the onions are translucent. Add the beans and stir. Add the garlic powder and paprika and cook for 3 minutes, or until the flavors combine.

2 Add the maple syrup, tomato sauce, 1 cup water, salt, and pepper. Stir to combine. Cook, stirring occasionally, for 20 minutes, or until the sauce thickens slightly. Add more water if needed for extra moisture.

CHICKPEA FRIES

MAKES: about 24 // **COOK TIME:** 20 minutes

Fries packed with protein, fiber, and magnesium sound almost too good to be true. *Almost.* These are a healthy alternative to deep-fried fries, and my kids devour them as though they are the real deal. The batter will get nice and thick while you whisk it on the stove—this is what you want for big steak-cut fries.

Coconut oil, for the pan

2 cups chickpea flour

4 cups chicken stock

½ teaspoon dried basil

⅛ teaspoon dried thyme

1 tablespoon chopped parsley

1 teaspoon lemon zest

1 tablespoon minced shallots

Pink Himalayan salt

Ground black pepper

1 cup olive oil

1 Grease a 9" × 13" sheet tray with raised edges with coconut oil.

2 In a medium saucepan over medium heat, add the flour, stock, basil, thyme, parsley, lemon zest, and shallots and cook, whisking continuously, for 5 minutes, or until the mixture thickens substantially. Season with salt and pepper. Spread the mixture evenly on the prepared sheet tray and refrigerate for 1 hour, or until firm.

3 Cut the mixture into large rectangles resembling the shape of thick-cut fries. Warm the olive oil in a large cast-iron pan over medium-high heat. Working in batches to not overcrowd the pan, fry each chickpea stick for 2 minutes on each side, or until golden brown and crispy. Remove from the pan and let dry on paper towels. Sprinkle with salt while they are still hot.

ZESTY QUINOA SALAD

SERVES: 4 // **COOK TIME:** 20 minutes

This recipe is a southwestern take on quinoa, with beans, cumin, and fresh lime juice. Make a double batch the night before when hosting a get-together or for bringing to a friend's house. The flavors combine the longer they sit and will have everyone saying "nom, nom."

1 cup quinoa

¼ cup olive oil

2 small limes, juiced

½ teaspoon lime zest

Pink Himalayan salt

2 teaspoons ground cumin

½ teaspoon red-pepper flakes

1 can (15 ounces) black beans, rinsed and drained

1½ cups cherry tomatoes, halved

1 tablespoon chopped parsley

5 green onions, white parts only, finely chopped

Ground black pepper

1 Cook the quinoa according to package directions. Let cool slightly.

2 In a small bowl, whisk together the oil, lime juice and zest, 1 teaspoon salt, the cumin, and pepper flakes until combined. In a large bowl, add the cooled quinoa, beans, tomatoes, parsley, and onions and mix together.

3 Pour the dressing over and toss to coat. Season with salt and pepper to taste. Serve immediately or chill.

LIME RICE

SERVES: 4 // **COOK TIME:** 35 minutes

I have such a love affair with rice. Growing up, I would eat white rice with butter and soy sauce—yikes! At least with brown rice, blood sugar won't spike, and it will leave you fuller longer. And while this probably didn't need an actual recipe, it's too good not to include. Ideal for elevating burrito bowls or any Mexican-inspired dish. Also, feel free to swap the butter for olive oil if you are staying away from dairy.

1 cup short-grain brown rice

¼ cup butter, divided

1½ tablespoons lime juice

1 teaspoon lime zest

1 teaspoon coarse sea salt

Cook the rice according to package directions with 2 tablespoons of the butter. In a large bowl, combine the cooked rice, lime juice and zest, salt, and the remaining 2 tablespoons butter.

LIMA BEAN DILL HASH

SERVES: 4 // **COOK TIME:** 15 minutes

Lima beans had a bad rep when I was growing up, and kids don't typically seem to be fans of them. Luckily, my kids will eat this recipe since it has a soft, sweet taste from dill plus other delicious veggies. This side dish is full of fiber, antioxidants, vitamins, and minerals.

1 teaspoon olive oil

1 large shallot, minced

½ cup chopped jarred red roasted bell peppers (about 1 large)

½ cup chopped cremini mushrooms

⅓ cup chopped asparagus

2 cups cooked lima beans

Pink Himalayan salt

3 tablespoons chopped dill

⅛ teaspoon lemon juice

1   In a medium skillet, heat the oil over medium-high heat. Add the shallot, bell peppers, mushrooms, and asparagus and sauté for 5 minutes, or until the asparagus is slightly tender.

2   Add the lima beans and a pinch of salt. Reduce the heat to medium-low and cook for 8 to 10 minutes, or until tender.

3   Remove from the heat and stir in the dill and lemon juice until combined. Serve warm.

NIBBLES

SPINACH AND ARTICHOKE DIP

MAKES: about 3 cups // **COOK TIME:** 35 minutes

I don't think anyone would argue that spinach artichoke dip is an all-time favorite of most people. I mean, what's not to love? A bowl full of cream with chunks of heavenly artichokes and spinach—you can't go wrong! That description sounds great, but my family's insides hate us after we indulge in that deliciousness. But not anymore: Skip the cream and go for rich coconut milk and sheep's milk yogurt so your digestive system (and waist) will thank you.

2 tablespoons olive oil, divided

1 onion, chopped

1 can (14 ounces) artichoke hearts, roughly chopped

1 tablespoon minced garlic

4 cups packed spinach

½ cup mayonnaise

¼ cup plain sheep's milk yogurt

¼ teaspoon pink Himalayan salt

¼ teaspoon ground black pepper

1 can (13.5 ounces) full-fat coconut milk or coconut cream

1 tablespoon arrowroot powder

1 Preheat the oven to 350°F.

2 In a large skillet, warm 1 tablespoon of the oil over medium-high heat. Add the onion and cook for 8 to 10 minutes, or until caramelized. Remove from the pan, place on a plate, and set aside.

3 In the same pan, sauté the artichokes and garlic over medium-low heat for 2 minutes. Add the spinach and cook for 3 minutes, stirring, or until wilted.

4 Stir in the mayo, yogurt, salt, and pepper. Scoop out the thick cream on top of the coconut milk (or about ¼ cup coconut cream) and add it to the same pan, discarding the coconut milk. Bring it to a boil.

5 In a small bowl, dissolve the arrowroot powder in 1 tablespoon water, stirring to combine. Add it to the spinach mixture over medium-low heat and stir until well combined. Add the onions and mix well.

6 Pour the mixture into an 8" × 8" baking dish and bake for 15 minutes. Turn the oven to broil and broil for 2 minutes. Let cool for 10 minutes before serving.

DATE DELIGHT BARS

MAKES: about 50 // **TOTAL TIME:** 2 hours 10 minutes

Since I'm constantly on the go, I'm always looking for a good bar to throw in my bag. I make my own trail mix with different nuts, dark chocolate chips, and either dried cherries or dates, so this is my trail mix turned into a bar. My kids love these just as much as I do.

½ cup coconut flakes

3 cups dates, pitted and roughly chopped

2½ cups raw walnuts, chopped

¼ cup + 1 tablespoon coconut oil, at room temperature

1 cup raw cacao nibs

1 cup coconut flour

½ cup creamy almond butter

Pinch of pink Himalayan salt

1 cup dark chocolate chips

1 Line a small baking sheet with parchment paper. In a food processor, pulse the coconut flakes and dates for 1 to 2 minutes, or until combined and it forms a ball.

2 In a large bowl, mix the walnuts, ¼ cup coconut oil, cacao nibs, coconut flour, almond butter, salt, and the date mixture together with your hands until well combined. It should form a pizza dough consistency.

3 Press the dough into the baking sheet, until about 1" thick. Chill in the fridge.

4 Using a bain-marie method (a hot water bath; see the note on page 205) or a double boiler, melt the chocolate chips and 1 tablespoon coconut oil together in a small glass bowl, stirring occasionally, until completely smooth.

5 Remove the baking sheet from the fridge and pour the melted chocolate over top, spreading evenly. Freeze for at least 1 hour or up to overnight.

6 Remove from the freezer and lift out of the baking sheet. Cut into 1" squares or small rectangles. Store in a resealable plastic bag in the fridge for up to 2 weeks or freezer for up to a month.

BLUEBERRY CASHEW BARS

MAKES: about 30 // **TOTAL TIME:** 2 hours 25 minutes

When I find my kids constantly going in the pantry (or, in this case, the fridge) for a snack I've made, then I know I have a hit on my hands. With creamy cashews, sweet dates, and blueberries, these bars remind me of my favorite blueberry Larabar. They're easy to grab and go and great to always have on hand.

2 cups roasted unsalted cashews

1 cup cashew butter

2 tablespoons hemp seeds

2 tablespoons coconut flakes

½ teaspoon vanilla bean powder

½ teaspoon ground cinnamon

1 cup dried blueberries

1 cup dates, pitted

1 cup raw almonds

1   Line a small baking sheet with parchment paper.

2   In a food processor, combine the cashews, cashew butter, hemp seeds, coconut flakes, vanilla powder, and cinnamon. Pulse until well combined. Press the mixture evenly into the baking sheet (should be about ¼ inch thick).

3   In the same food processor, add the blueberries, dates, and almonds. Pulse for 3 minutes, or until combined and you are able to form a sticky ball with your hands and the almonds are finely chopped.

4   Place the blueberry mixture on top of the cashew mixture in the baking sheet. Firmly push the fruit mixture toward the edges to evenly distribute it, completely covering the cashew crust, being careful not to move the cashew mixture too much.

5   Chill in the freezer for at least 2 hours or up to overnight. Cut into small bars, then store in the fridge for up to 2 weeks or in the freezer for up to a month.

CANNELLINI BEAN AND PISTACHIO HUMMUS

MAKES: about 3 cups // **TOTAL TIME:** 10 minutes

Kristin and I share some similarities, but the biggest is that we're both Italian. We like to incorporate this into dishes or foods that aren't typically Italian, such as this light and creamy play on hummus. The flavors are subtle and refreshing. **–MIKE**

2½ cups canned cannellini beans

1 clove garlic

½ cup shelled dry-roasted pistachios

2 tablespoons champagne vinegar

2 tablespoons flat-leaf parsley

1 tablespoon tahini

2 teaspoons fresh lemon juice

1 teaspoon lemon zest

1 teaspoon cumin

1½ teaspoons pink Himalayan salt

½ cup + 1 tablespoon olive oil

In a food processor, combine the beans, garlic, pistachios, vinegar, parsley, tahini, lemon juice and zest, cumin, and salt. Blend on high until smooth. With the food processor running, drizzle in the oil until fully combined and emulsified into paste. Keeps well in the fridge for up to a week.

ARTICHOKE HUMMUS

MAKES: about 3 cups // **TOTAL TIME:** 10 minutes

The best hummus I've ever eaten was from a small farmers' market in LA. There was a station set up with every kind of hummus imaginable, but the one I found myself dreaming about long after I had it was the artichoke hummus. It was incredibly creamy yet light, with just the right amount of artichoke flavor. Now, I can do more than just dream of it: I give you artichoke hummus that is just as good as the farmers' market one—*maybe* even better. Eat with veggies, a healthy chip, or on sandwiches or wraps in place of mayo.

2½ cups canned chickpeas

½ cup fresh basil

1 cup artichoke hearts

½ teaspoon lemon zest

1 teaspoon lemon juice

1 tablespoon Roasted Garlic (page 223)

1 tablespoon white wine vinegar

¼ cup olive oil

1 teaspoon pink Himalayan salt

Place the chickpeas in a food processor and blend until smooth. Add the basil, artichoke hearts, lemon zest and juice, garlic, and vinegar. Blend until well combined. With the food processor running, slowly drizzle in the oil. Add the salt and mix until the hummus is a smooth, creamy texture. Keeps well in the fridge for up to a week.

BASIC BEEF JERKY

MAKES: 2 pounds // **COOK TIME:** 3 hours

What's not to love about beef jerky? It has great flavor, is full of protein, and is an easy, transportable snack. My friends often make fun of me because I typically have a small bag of homemade beef jerky in my purse to snack on. Once you get the hang of this basic recipe, the sky's the limit as to what marinades you can create. Slice your beef to the size and thickness of jerky you prefer. I love my dehydrator and would recommend getting one, but it's not required.

¾ cup Worcestershire sauce

⅓ cup tamari

1 tablespoon smoked paprika

2 tablespoons raw honey

2 teaspoons lemon pepper

1 teaspoon chopped parsley

1 teaspoon red-pepper flakes (optional)

1 teaspoon minced garlic

½ teaspoon ground turmeric

2 pounds beef sirloin, thinly sliced

1   In a small bowl, combine the Worcestershire sauce, tamari, paprika, honey, lemon pepper, parsley, pepper flakes (if using), garlic, and turmeric.

2   Place the sirloin in a resealable plastic bag or baking dish and pour the marinade over it to coat. Marinate in the refrigerator for at least 1 hour or up to overnight.

3   Preheat the oven to 170°F or a dehydrator to 155°F to 160°F.

4   Remove the meat from the marinade and place on a large baking sheet. Cook in the oven for 3 hours, flipping halfway through, or 3 to 4 hours in the dehydrator. Remove once the beef is a soft, leatherlike consistency. It will harden slightly as it cools. Keeps well in a resealable plastic bag or airtight container on the counter for 2 days or in the fridge for up to a week.

ZUCCHINI CHIPS WITH DILL SOUR CREAM AND ONION DIP

MAKES: about 50 chips // **COOK TIME:** 40 minutes

I've made every kind of chip: apple, beet, carrot, you name it. I decided to include this recipe for zucchini chips for two reasons: They pair well with the sour cream and onion dip, but more importantly, you get the satisfaction of eating a "chip" while getting some greens in. How can you not love that? Once you master these, try this recipe using apples, beets, or carrots.

1 medium zucchini, thinly sliced on a mandoline

Olive oil

Pink Himalayan salt

Ground black pepper

1 cup oat flour

Dill Sour Cream and Onion Dip (page 144)

1 Lay out the zucchini slices in a single layer on paper towels. Cover with another paper towel and place a baking sheet on top (for the weight) to draw out moisture. Let sit for 1 hour.

2 Preheat the oven to 350°F. Line a large baking sheet with parchment paper and brush with oil.

3 Remove the baking sheet and paper towels from the zucchini. Sprinkle with salt and pepper. In a sink or over a garbage bin, place the zucchini in a large colander and pour the oat flour on top. Shake the colander until each piece of zucchini is well coated.

4 Evenly place the zucchini slices on the prepared baking sheet. Bake for 40 minutes, rotating pan halfway through, or until crispy. Let cool slightly and serve with the Dill Sour Cream and Onion Dip.

RECIPE CONTINUES

DILL SOUR CREAM AND ONION DIP

MAKES: about 2 cups // **COOK TIME:** 15 minutes

¼ cup olive oil

1 large yellow onion, finely minced

1 shallot, finely minced

1 clove garlic, minced

1 teaspoon Worcestershire sauce

2 tablespoons chopped dill

2 cups plain sheep's milk yogurt

Pinch of ground black pepper

½ teaspoon celery salt

1 teaspoon chopped parsley (optional)

1   Warm the oil in a medium skillet over medium heat. Add the onion and shallot and sauté for 5 minutes. Add the garlic and sauté for 8 to 10 minutes, or until the onions are caramelized. Remove from the heat.

2   In a medium bowl, whisk together the Worcestershire sauce, dill, yogurt, pepper, and celery salt. Fold in the onion mixture. Let sit in the refrigerator for at least 1 hour or up to overnight. Garnish with the parsley (if using) and serve with zucchini chips.

BAY SCALLOP SEVICHE WITH PLANTAIN CHIPS

MAKES: 2–3 cups // **COOK TIME:** 35 minutes

Seviche reminds me of sitting on the beach somewhere warm. One of my favorite lunches, this is refreshing while bringing tons of flavor. Make this the night before and let it marinate in the fridge overnight, or, if you don't have that much time, just let it sit for an hour. It makes a delicious lunch for two or is great to have out as an appetizer for family or friends to nibble on when hosting. In a time crunch, skip the multiple marinades.

1 pound bay scallops

⅛ teaspoon pink Himalayan salt

1 tablespoon lime juice

1 lime, zested

⅓ cup fresh orange juice

½ shallot, sliced

½ cup diced red bell peppers

1 tablespoon fresh lemon juice

½ cup roasted corn

½ cup halved grape tomatoes

2 tablespoons chopped parsley

1 large plantain, peeled

Olive oil

1 avocado, cubed

1   Place the scallops in a colander and rinse with cold water until the bubbles disperse. Place in a medium bowl and sprinkle with the salt. Add the lime juice and zest, orange juice, and shallot and mix well. Marinate in the refrigerator for 1 hour or up to overnight.

2   In a medium bowl, mix the bell peppers, lemon juice, corn, tomatoes, and parsley. Combine with the scallops and let sit in the refrigerator for 2 hours or up to overnight.

3   Meanwhile, preheat the oven to 350°F. Line a large baking sheet with foil.

4   Thinly slice the plantain using a mandoline. Coat each slice with oil and lay on the baking sheet. Sprinkle each with a pinch of salt and bake for 35 minutes, or until golden brown and crispy.

5   When ready to eat, mix the avocado with the seviche and serve immediately with the plantain chips.

SPICY ENDIVE TUNA BITES

MAKES: about 18 // **COOK TIME:** 2 minutes

My boys *love* sushi. Yes, you read that right: They go crazy for it. I got them started on it young, and now they literally cheer when we get it. They haven't come to the spicy side yet, so when I make these, I leave a little tuna out for their own non-spicy bites. I, on the other hand, live for spicy tuna. It's the first roll I order at any sushi restaurant. I've been making spicy tuna for years, long before I even considered myself able to cook. It's easy and oh so good.

1 pound fresh ahi tuna, cubed

1 teaspoon sesame oil

1 teaspoon black sesame seeds + more for garnish

2 tablespoons chopped scallions

Pink Himalayan salt

½ lime, juiced

¼ cup mayonnaise

¼ cup Sriracha sauce

3 heads Belgium endives

1 teaspoon olive oil

Ground black pepper

Micro-greens for garnish (optional)

1   In the food processor, add tuna, sesame oil, sesame seeds, scallions, and a pinch of salt. Pulse until the tuna is bite-size. Place the mixture in a large bowl and set aside.

2   In a small bowl, mix the lime juice, mayonnaise, and Sriracha until combined. Pour over the tuna and coat it thoroughly. Chill for 30 minutes in the fridge.

3   Warm a skillet over high heat. Cut the endives in half lengthwise, keeping the stems, and brush with the olive oil and season with salt and pepper. When the pan is hot, sear the endives facedown for 45 seconds on each side, until slightly charred. Let the endives cool, then pull each piece apart.

4   Scoop the tuna mixture into the endive boats. Garnish with sesame seeds and micro-greens (if using).

KIDS' FAVORITE FRITTERS

MAKES: about 20 // **COOK TIME:** 10 minutes

My kids love Dr. Praeger's Broccoli Littles, so here is our homemade version. These will last in the freezer up to a month and are a great, healthy snack—packed with a ton of greens—to have on hand for the kiddos. I've even been known to eat a couple.

1 medium zucchini, grated

1 small head broccoli, finely chopped

1 scallion, chopped

1 clove garlic, minced

¼ cup chopped parsley

1 teaspoon chopped dill

½ teaspoon lemon juice

½ teaspoon Pink Himalayan salt

½ cup oat flour

1 teaspoon baking powder

2 eggs

Olive oil

1   Wrap the grated zucchini in paper towels or cheesecloth and squeeze out extra moisture, making sure to get out as much as possible. Place in a medium bowl. Add the broccoli, scallion, garlic, parsley, dill, lemon juice, and the salt. Stir to combine.

2   In a separate bowl, whisk together the oat flour, baking powder, and eggs while adding up to ¼ cup water, a little at a time, until you have a smooth consistency (you don't want the batter to be runny).

3   Pour the batter into the vegetable mixture, folding to combine. Add 1 to 2 tablespoons more of the flour if the batter seems too runny.

4   Warm ¼ cup olive oil in a medium skillet over medium-high heat. Working in batches to not overcrowd the pan, spoon about 1½ tablespoons of the mixture for each fritter in the oil. (You may need a little more oil to fry the fritters depending on how many batches you do.) Fry for 2 to 3 minutes, or until golden brown. Flip the fritters and fry for another 2 to 3 minutes, or until completely golden brown and the fitters have set. Remove and allow to cool on a paper towel. Sprinkle with salt. Store in the fridge for up to a week or in the freezer for up to a month.

GOAT CHEESE–STUFFED JALAPEÑOS

MAKES: 24 // **COOK TIME:** 15 minutes

These are a better-for-you jalapeño popper—and if you've ever had one of those, then you know they are dangerously addictive. I grew up eating them but haven't gone near one since I started eating better years ago. Make these when you need to bring an appetizer to a BBQ or when you just want to win points with your man.

---

12 jalapeño chile peppers, halved lengthwise, seeds and ribs removed (be careful when handling)

10 ounces goat cheese

8 cloves Roasted Garlic (page 223), minced

⅔ cup pine nuts, chopped

6 sprigs thyme, roughly chopped

1   Preheat the oven to 425°F.

2   Arrange the chile peppers, cut side down, on a baking sheet. Roast for 5 minutes, or until tender. Let cool 5 minutes, until warm to the touch.

3   Meanwhile, in a medium bowl, mix the goat cheese and garlic with your hands, making sure the garlic is evenly incorporated. In another small bowl, mix together the pine nuts and thyme.

4   Press a generous amount of the cheese mixture into 1 chile pepper half, until just overflowing. Press the cheese side of the pepper in the pine nut mixture until well coated, then place on a baking sheet, cheese side up. Repeat with the remaining peppers.

5   Bake for 5 minutes, or until the cheese begins to melt and the pine nuts turn golden. Turn the oven to broil, and cook for another 2 to 3 minutes, or until slightly golden brown.

STRAWBERRY-MANGO FRUIT ROLL-UPS

MAKES: about 16 // **COOK TIME:** 5 hours

I spent my entire childhood eating fruit roll-ups—I can only imagine the chemicals in those things. I make these roll-ups, or fruit leather, on parchment paper so the kids can have the same experience I did of pulling them off the paper. I only wish I had about 20 ovens so I could make bigger batches since they are gone within a day.

2 cups strawberries, halved

1 large mango, cubed

2 tablespoons raw honey

1 tablespoon orange juice

1   Preheat the oven to 200°F. Line 2 small baking sheets with parchment paper.

2   In a blender, puree the strawberries, mango, honey, and orange juice until well combined and it has a souplike consistency. Evenly spread the mixture in the lined baking sheets with a spatula, making sure to spread all the way to the edges. Bake for 5 hours, turning the pans halfway through, until the leather is no longer sticky or gooey (check the middle).

3   Let cool. Then, using scissors, cut into long strips and roll up with the parchment paper on the back.

FIG AND ZUCCHINI ROLL-UPS

MAKES: about 25 // **COOK TIME:** 40 minutes

This was one of the first appetizers I ever came up with. While looking through cooking magazines, I came across another zucchini roll-up. I got inspired and decided to put a few of my favorite things together and created roll-up-bliss. Goat cheese meshed with an orange-fig jam and rolled up in a healthy zucchini strip is all I need for finger-food happiness. They're great for any gathering—put a toothpick in each one so people can just pop them in their mouths.

1 cup dried Mission figs

¼ cup raw honey

1 orange, zested

¼ cup fresh orange juice

1 sprig rosemary, chopped

¼ teaspoon ground black pepper

Pink Himalayan salt

2 large (or 3 small) zucchini, sliced thinly on a mandoline

4 ounces goat cheese crumbles

½ cup chopped walnuts

1 Preheat the oven to 400°F.

2 Place the figs in a food processor and pulse until finely chopped. In a small saucepan, combine the figs, honey, orange zest and juice, rosemary, and pepper and bring to a boil. Reduce the heat, cover, and simmer for 8 minutes, stirring occasionally, or until the figs are tender. Uncover and cook for another 5 to 8 minutes, or until thick and jamlike. Remove from the heat. Stir in ½ teaspoon salt and let cool 10 minutes.

3 Lay out the zucchini strips. Place about 1 teaspoon of the jam and a few crumbles of goat cheese on one end of a zucchini strip. Roll the zucchini tightly and use a toothpick to hold it together. Place seam side down in a baking dish. Repeat with the remaining zucchini, jam, and goat cheese. Sprinkle each with a big pinch of salt.

4 Bake for 15 minutes. Remove and sprinkle the roll-ups with the walnuts. Place the baking dish back in the oven and bake for 5 minutes. Let cool slightly before serving.

PICK-ME-UPS

GOLDEN MILK

SERVES: 1 // **TOTAL TIME:** 5 minutes

The first time I had Golden Milk was at a juice shop in LA. Since I was living in Chicago at the time, I knew I had to re-create it to be able to get my fix. It's loaded with healthy spices, such as turmeric and cinnamon (both anti-inflammatory), and tastes like an incredible glass of spiced creamy milk.

1 cup Cashew Milk (page 217)

¼ teaspoon ground turmeric

⅛ teaspoon ground cardamom

¼ teaspoon ground cinnamon

¼ teaspoon vanilla powder

1 teaspoon pure maple syrup

Whisk together the milk, turmeric, cardamom, cinnamon, vanilla, and maple syrup until well combined. Serve chilled or over ice.

SPANISH SPICED LATTE

SERVES: 1 // **TOTAL TIME:** 10 minutes

This heavenly drink is a comforting latte with a little kick—right up my alley. Drink it warm (my fave), or cool it down and serve over ice.

1 tablespoon raw cocoa powder

¼ teaspoon ground cinnamon

¼ teaspoon ground nutmeg

⅛ teaspoon cayenne pepper

6 ounces freshly brewed black coffee

1 tablespoon pure maple syrup

2 tablespoons coconut cream

In a small bowl, mix the cocoa powder, cinnamon, nutmeg, and pepper. Add the coffee and maple syrup and stir to combine. Transfer to a large mug and whisk in the coconut cream.

HONEY TURMERIC LATTE

SERVES: 1 // **TOTAL TIME:** 10 minutes

Honey and turmeric make this latte sweet and savory. Anti-inflammatory from turmeric, and antibacterial and antifungal from raw honey, this is packed with tons of health benefits.

1 cup Cashew Milk (page 217)

¼ cup canned full-fat coconut milk

1–2 shots espresso

1 tablespoon raw honey

⅛ teaspoon ground turmeric

In a small saucepan over medium-high heat, warm the cashew and coconut milk together until desired temperature. Pour in a high-powered blender and add the espresso, honey, and turmeric. Blend on high for 30 seconds, or until well combined and slightly frothy. Pour in a mug and serve immediately.

MACA MOCHA

SERVES: 1 // **TOTAL TIME:** 10 minutes

Maca is a root vegetable considered a superfood for its incredible health benefits. It's packed with more than 20 amino acids, tons of vitamins and minerals, and plenty of phytonutrients. It's also known to boost sex drive. Hey, why not!

1 cup Cashew Milk (page 217)

1–2 shots espresso

2 teaspoons pure maple syrup

1 teaspoon maca powder

1 teaspoon raw cacao powder

¼ teaspoon vanilla powder

In a small saucepan, warm the milk to desired temperature. Place in a high-powered blender with the espresso, maple syrup, maca powder, cacao powder, and vanilla. Blend on high for 30 seconds, or until frothy.

ICED CARAMEL LATTE

SERVES: 1 // **TOTAL TIME:** 5 minutes

In my early twenties, an iced caramel latte was my almost-daily order at Starbucks. I would make sure I got every last drop of caramel, aka sugar sugar sugar. Here is a much healthier version made without refined sugar. If you don't want it super sweet, use half the caramel.

4 tablespoons Caramel Sauce, divided (page 232)

1–2 shots espresso, chilled

½ cup canned full-fat coconut milk

Place 2 tablespoons of the caramel in the bottom of a tall glass. Put 1 to 2 handfuls of ice on top of the caramel, then pour the espresso over top. Add the milk followed by the remaining 2 tablespoons caramel.

COCONUT LATTE

SERVES: 1 // **TOTAL TIME:** 10 minutes

If you follow me on social media, then you've definitely seen me make these. My go-to coffee, this is rich and creamy and all I need to get my day going.

1 cup canned full-fat coconut milk

1–2 shots espresso

1 teaspoon pure maple syrup

½ teaspoon pure vanilla extract

In a saucepan over medium heat, warm the coconut milk to desired temperature. Place the milk, espresso, maple syrup, and vanilla in a high-powered blender and blend on high for 20 seconds, or until frothy. Pour in a mug and enjoy right away.

CACAO CASHEW MILK WITH SPIRULINA

SERVES: 1 // **TOTAL TIME:** 5 minutes

Spirulina (blue-green algae) is loaded with protein, iron, beta-carotene, vitamins, and minerals. The cacao milk hides the otherwise bold flavor, making it easy to get the nutrients down. I started making this to get spirulina in my kids, and to this day, it never fails.

1½ cups Cacao Cashew Milk (page 218)

⅛ teaspoon spirulina powder

Place the milk and spirulina in a large glass and whisk to combine. Enjoy.

POWER MATCHA LATTE

SERVES: 1 // **TOTAL TIME:** 10 minutes

I don't drink coffee every day, and because of that, it really affects me when I do. If I drink it past noon, it will take me forever to fall asleep that night. But having three little kids means I usually need an afternoon pick-me-up, and that's why I love matcha. It doesn't have as much caffeine as coffee, so I can still fall asleep come bedtime, but it gives a good energy boost. Just like coffee blended with butter and brain-octane oil (to boost cognitive performance and aid in weight loss), this energizing matcha will get you going and won't leave you with a crash.

1 cup plain Almond Milk (page 216)

1 teaspoon matcha powder

1 tablespoon coconut oil or butter

5–8 drops liquid stevia

¼ teaspoon vanilla extract

In a small saucepan over medium-high heat, whisk together the milk and matcha until well combined and temperature is to your liking. Place in a high-powered blender and add the oil, stevia, and vanilla. Blend on high for 30 seconds, or until frothy.

BLENDED MOCHA

SERVES: 1 // **TOTAL TIME:** 5 minutes

During the spring and summer, I drink a smoothie almost every morning. They're refreshing and such an easy way to get in a ton of nutrients. This particular smoothie gives a good coffee jolt to start your day and is creamy with frozen banana and avocado, resembling a yummy coffee milkshake.

¾ cup plain Almond Milk (page 216)

½ cup chilled coffee

1 tablespoon almond butter

1 teaspoon raw cocoa powder

1 small frozen banana

½ frozen avocado (regular works too)

1 teaspoon raw honey

Pinch of pink Himalayan salt

In a high-powered blender, place the milk, coffee, almond butter, cocoa powder, banana, avocado, honey, and salt. Blend on high until smooth.

MINTY MATCHA SMOOTHIE

SERVES: 1 // **TOTAL TIME:** 5 minutes

I have a weakness for anything peppermint (especially mint chocolate), and this smoothie reminds me of cooling mint ice cream. Matcha gives a little energy boost, perfect in the morning, as an afternoon pick-me-up, or even as a refreshing dessert.

1½ frozen bananas

½ teaspoon matcha powder

⅛ teaspoon peppermint extract

1 cup plain Almond, Cashew, or Pecan Milk (page 216, 217, or 220)

In a high-powered blender, place the bananas, matcha, peppermint, and milk. Blend on high until well combined.

ICED MATCHA LATTE

SERVES: 1 // **TOTAL TIME:** 10 minutes

Perfect over ice to cool down during the warm summer months while running around outside with the kids.

1 cup plain Almond Milk (page 216)

1 teaspoon matcha powder

1 teaspoon pure maple syrup

¼ teaspoon vanilla extract

2 tablespoons canned full-fat coconut milk

¼ teaspoon ground cinnamon

1 In a small saucepan over medium-high heat, whisk together the Almond Milk, matcha, maple syrup, and vanilla until well combined and the temperature is to your liking.

2 Add a handful of ice to a large glass. Give the matcha mixture a good stir to make sure the powder didn't sink to the bottom, then pour in the glass. Drizzle in the coconut milk and sprinkle the cinnamon on top.

CREAMY CINNAMON SMOOTHIE

SERVES: 1 // **TOTAL TIME:** 10 minutes

This smoothie is more about the light, fluffy creaminess than the cinnamon, which is subtle. I debated whether to include this smoothie because while I like it, I didn't know how many other people would make a cinnamon smoothie on the regular. But when I asked Jay, he said, "It's too good not to." So here ya go. Plus, cinnamon is a powerful antioxidant and reduces inflammation.

1½ frozen bananas

1 cup plain Almond, Cashew, or Pecan Milk (page 216, 217, or 220)

1 tablespoon creamy almond butter

1 teaspoon raw honey

¼ teaspoon ground cinnamon

1 teaspoon maca powder

In a high-powered blender, place the bananas, milk, almond butter, honey, cinnamon, and maca. Blend on high until smooth and well combined.

SHOULD-BE-DESSERT SMOOTHIE

SERVES: 1 // **TOTAL TIME:** 5 minutes

I drink this when I have the urge for a milkshake—it can easily pass for one. I threw frozen cauliflower in here so there's some good nutritional value (in addition to the vitamins and minerals from the greens powder), and it only adds to the creamy deliciousness to make this a should-be-dessert smoothie. Just make sure to steam your cauliflower before freezing it. You're welcome.

2 frozen bananas

¼ cup frozen cauliflower (steam before freezing)

2 scoops chocolate greens, such as Amazing Grass Green Superfood

2 tablespoons raw honey

2 tablespoons raw cacao nibs

1 can (13.5 ounces) full-fat coconut milk

In a high-powered blender, place the bananas, cauliflower, chocolate greens, honey, cacao nibs, and milk. Blend on high until combined. Serve immediately.

SMOOTHIE BOWLS

I know something is a huge trend when I see it popping up places other than LA, and smoothie bowls are really having a moment. They're a nice change from ordinary smoothies and are more of a filling meal. I try to always throw a green in mine so I can check off a serving. Smoothie bowls are best eaten with a spoon, but you can sip yours like you would normally drink a smoothie.

CHOCOLATE CRUNCH SMOOTHIE BOWL

SERVES: 1 // **TOTAL TIME:** 15 minutes

2 frozen bananas

1 tablespoon raw cocoa powder

1 teaspoon maca powder

1 cup plain Almond, Cashew, or Pecan Milk (page 216, 217, or 220)

1 tablespoon almond butter

1 tablespoon cacao nibs

1 tablespoon raw honey

1 cup packed spinach

3 tablespoons chopped cherries

½ tablespoon black sesame seeds

2 tablespoons sliced raw almonds

In a high-powered blender, place the bananas, cocoa powder, maca, milk, almond butter, cacao nibs, honey, and spinach. Blend on high until well combined. Pour in a small bowl and top with the cherries, sesame seeds, and almonds or your favorite toppings.

GREEN SMOOTHIE BOWL

SERVES: 1 // **TOTAL TIME:** 15 minutes

1 frozen banana

1 cup spinach

¼ teaspoon spirulina powder

½ avocado, peeled and pit removed

2 teaspoons raw honey

1 tablespoon hemp seeds

1 cup plain Almond, Cashew, or Pecan Milk (page 216, 217, or 220)

1 teaspoon vanilla extract

3–4 strawberries, sliced

½ banana, sliced

1 tablespoon cacao nibs

In a high-powered blender, place the frozen banana, spinach, spirulina, avocado, honey, hemp seeds, milk, and vanilla. Blend on high until well combined. Pour in a small bowl and top with the strawberries, sliced banana, and cacao nibs or your favorite toppings.

VANILLA BERRY SMOOTHIE BOWL

SERVES: 1 // **TOTAL TIME:** 15 minutes

¼ cup frozen blackberries

1 frozen banana

¼ cup blueberries

2 tablespoons creamy almond butter

1 teaspoon raw honey

½ teaspoon vanilla bean powder or pure vanilla extract

1¼ cups plain Almond, Cashew, or Pecan Milk (page 216, 217, or 220)

1 tablespoon bee pollen

1 tablespoon hemp seeds

4 strawberries, sliced

In a high-powered blender, place the blackberries, banana, blueberries, almond butter, honey, vanilla, and milk. Blend on high until well combined. Pour in a small bowl and top with the bee pollen, hemp seeds, and strawberries or your favorite toppings.

FRESH JUICES

We all know by now that fresh juices are good for us. I can easily drink an entire juice made from just greens, but most people—aka my kids—need apple or another fruit to round out the bitterness and bring in a sweet element. For them, it's no fruit, no juice. So in honor of my kids, I give you our favorite juice combos that have been perfectly sweetened.

SWEET GREENS

SERVES: 1 // **TOTAL TIME:** 10 minutes

1 red apple, core removed

1 pear, ends trimmed and seeds removed

½ cucumber

2 stalks celery

2 cups packed spinach

In a juicer or high-powered blender, place the apple, pear, cucumber, celery, and spinach. Juice or blend until well combined. Serve immediately.

THE REFRESHER

SERVES: 1 // **TOTAL TIME:** 15 minutes

1 cup loosely packed mint leaves

1 small honeydew melon or ½ large honeydew melon, skin removed and cut into ¼" pieces

1 cucumber, halved

2 cups packed spinach

1 teaspoon aloe juice

In a juicer or high-powered blender, place the mint, melon, cucumber, and spinach. Juice or blend until well combined. Pour into a glass and stir in the aloe. Serve immediately.

BERRY DETOX JUICE

SERVES: 1 // **TOTAL TIME:** 15 minutes

2 cups strawberries, green parts removed

2 beets, ends trimmed and halved

3 stalks celery

½" piece ginger, peeled

1 lemon, peeled

In a juicer or high-powered blender, place the strawberries, beets, celery, ginger, and lemon. Juice or blend until well combined. Enjoy immediately.

APPLE CIDER FIGHTER

SERVES: 1 // **TOTAL TIME:** 5 minutes

I swear by this concoction: Anytime I feel a cold coming on or just feel a little off, I drink this and almost immediately feel better. Apple cider vinegar truly does it all. It eases upset stomachs, soothes sore throats, prevents indigestion, boosts energy, helps control blood sugar—the list goes on and on. Ginger and lemon also help fight colds and alkalize the body.

4 Ginger-Infused Ice Cubes (page 236)

1 ounce apple cider vinegar

1 ounce fresh lemon juice

16 ounces sparkling water

Place the ginger ice cubes in a tall glass. Pour the vinegar, lemon juice, and sparkling water on top. Stir.

BOTTOMS UP

FIZZY SPICY MARGARITA

SERVES: 1 // **TOTAL TIME:** 10 minutes

This delicious little baby is my go-to drink and is one of the best drinks *for* you (at least on the alcohol scale, since blanco tequila is the most unprocessed alcohol). A skinny, spicy marg, it's light and fresh with a nice little kick. I get hungover very easily these days, and I swear this is the only drink that won't put me out the next day. Enjoy!

1.5 ounces silver tequila

1 ounce fresh lime juice

0.5 ounce pure maple syrup

6 ounces sparkling water

½–1 jalapeño chile pepper, seeded and sliced (be careful when handling)

In a glass, stir together tequila, lime juice, maple syrup, sparkling water, and chile pepper. Place a handful of ice over top and stir. You could also blend this up with ice and garnish with extra chile peppers for a frozen margarita instead.

G&G (GIN AND GINGER)

SERVES: 1 // **TOTAL TIME:** 10 minutes

Ginger was made for gin—they go together like eggs and bacon, peanut butter and jelly, blah blah blah . . . you get it. Perfect cocktail harmony.

---

2 ounces gin

1 ounce fresh ginger juice

2 ounces sparkling water

1 lime wedge

Using a martini shaker, shake the gin and ginger juice together for about 20 seconds. Pour over ice and add the sparkling water. Squeeze the juice from the lime into the drink, then put the rind on the glass to garnish.

ROSÉ SANGRIA

MAKES: about 7 cups // **TOTAL TIME:** 45 minutes

I'm currently obsessed with rosé. Yeah, me and everybody else. I love this take on classic sangria—it's light, fresh, and sweet. Make a pitcher for a gathering, especially on a warm summer afternoon while outside barbecuing, if possible.

3 cups sliced strawberries, divided

1 diced mango (about 1 cup), divided

½ cup chopped basil

8 ounces cranberry- or raspberry-flavored sparkling water

8 ounces raspberry-flavored vodka

1 bottle sparkling rosé

1   In a high-powered blender, combine 2 cups of the strawberries and $1/2$ cup of the mango and blend until pureed. Strain the mixture into a large pitcher, using a spoon or spatula to press down on the mixture to get as much juice out as possible. Discard the pulp.

2   Add the basil, sparkling water, vodka, rosé, and the remaining 1 cup strawberries and $1/2$ cup mango to the pitcher. Stir to combine. Chill for 30 minutes or up to 2 hours. Serve over ice.

BLOODHOUND WITH THYME

SERVES: 1 // **TOTAL TIME:** 10 minutes

Greyhounds—aka grapefruit and vodka—have been a favorite of mine since I started drinking alcohol (no, I'm not going to say what age that was). They're refreshing and oh-so-yummy with fresh grapefruit juice (I've changed the name slightly since I use ruby red grapefruit). I like adding a little sparkling water for some bubbles, and it means you're hydrating at the same time, right?!

2 ounces vodka

4 ounces fresh ruby red grapefruit juice

2 sprigs thyme

2 ounces sparkling water

Using a martini shaker, shake the vodka, grapefruit juice, and thyme together with a handful of ice. Using a cheesecloth or strainer, strain the mixture into a chilled glass over ice. Pour the sparkling water over and stir to combine.

AN EVEN BETTER BLOODY MARY

SERVES: 1 // **TOTAL TIME:** 8 hours 10 minutes

With a ton of depth and flavor, this is no ordinary bloody since it's made with infused vodka. We came up with this recipe when Mike suggested infusing the vodka to make it that much better, and boy was he right. Just know that infusing vodka takes at least a day, so you'll want to do that the day before you want your bloodies.

2 ounces Infused Vodka (see below)

4 ounces tomato juice

½ teaspoon minced garlic

1 teaspoon Worcestershire sauce

½–1 teaspoon Sriracha sauce, depending on preference

½ teaspoon celery salt

Pinch of ground black pepper

0.4 ounce fresh lemon juice

3 green Spanish olives

2 cooked bacon strips

1 stalk celery heart

1 lemon slice

In a large mason jar, add the vodka, tomato juice, garlic, Worcestershire sauce, Sriracha, celery salt, pepper, and lemon juice. Shake until combined, then pour into a cup over ice. Serve with the olives and bacon on a skewer, along with the celery stick and lemon slice.

INFUSED VODKA

1 bottle vodka

½ teaspoon horseradish

¼ teaspoon red-pepper flakes

1 teaspoon dill seeds

1 clove garlic, halved

2 canned fire-roasted Roma tomatoes

½ teaspoon whole black peppercorns

1 lemon wedge

Pinch of celery salt

In a large mason jar or pitcher, place the vodka, horseradish, pepper flakes, dill, garlic, tomatoes, peppercorns, and lemon. Cover and shake well. Place in the fridge for 8 hours or up to overnight, occasionally shaking. Strain the mixture through a fine strainer.

SUMMER MIMOSA

SERVES: 1 // **TOTAL TIME:** 10 minutes

This is a fun take on the traditional brunch bubbly (and good any time of day!). Skip the prosciutto-wrapped cantaloupe balls to save time—they definitely aren't needed, just enjoyable.

7 ounces dry Prosecco

3 ounces fresh cantaloupe juice

1 small piece cantaloupe, balled (about 3–4 balls)

1 piece prosciutto

Pour the Prosecco into a champagne glass. Slowly add the cantaloupe juice, stirring. Put the cantaloupe balls on a long skewer, wrap the prosciutto around them, and place in the glass to garnish.

JAY'S WHISKEY

SERVES: 1 // **TOTAL TIME:** 10 minutes

This recipe is for Jay, my whiskey man. I won't go near the stuff; it's not my cup of tea. Whiskey is pretty much all Jay drinks, though, so here is a nice twist on ordinary whiskey on the rocks.

2 ounces aged whiskey

3 Ginger-Infused Ice Cubes (page 236)

1 sprig thyme

Pour the whiskey in a glass and add the ginger ice cubes. Let sit for 5 minutes, until the ice cubes melt slightly. Stir to combine. Garnish with the thyme.

LAST BUT NOT LEAST

BANANA TURNOVER CAKE

SERVES: 6–8 // **COOK TIME:** 50 minutes

Think of this as caramelized bananas baked into a dense yellow cake, then glazed with sugar. Yeah, it's really good. Even my chocolate-loving husband and kids think this cake is amazing.

---

7 ripe bananas, 2 sliced, divided

3 eggs

½ cup coconut oil, melted

½ cup coconut sugar

¼ teaspoon cardamom

2 teaspoons ground cinnamon

2 cups oat flour

½ cup coconut shortening

½ cup pure maple syrup

1 Preheat the oven to 350°F.

2 In a large bowl, mash together the 5 whole bananas, the eggs, oil, sugar, cardamom, and cinnamon until well combined. Stir in the oat flour until the batter comes together without any flour lumps.

3 In a medium cast-iron skillet over low heat, whisk the coconut shortening and maple syrup until well combined. Increase the heat to medium and cook for 3 to 5 minutes, or until the mixture starts to thicken and bubble. Pour into an 8" × 8" baking dish.

4 Lay the 2 sliced bananas in a single layer on top of the maple caramel. Gently scoop the batter over the bananas and caramel, evenly distributing it and being careful not to move the bananas too much. Spread to even out.

5 Bake for 40 to 45 minutes, or until a toothpick comes out clean. Remove and let cool completely before flipping over onto a platter or cutting board.

ZUCCHINI ALMOND BUTTER BLONDIES

MAKES: about 16 // **COOK TIME:** 30 minutes

I went back and forth about what to call this little creation. I was thinking of calling it one big-ass cookie, because it reminds me of a "pizookie" (one giant warm cookie with vanilla ice cream on top), which I used to always get from a restaurant in Laguna Beach. But I ultimately decided that these are in fact blondies. And let me just say, these are about to change your life because you're going to discover that dessert can taste amazing and be somewhat good for you (and you can't taste the zucchini at all—it just makes these super moist).

1 cup creamy almond butter

1 egg

½ teaspoon pink Himalayan salt

½ teaspoon baking soda

½ cup coconut sugar

½ teaspoon pure vanilla extract

½ cup dark chocolate chips

1 large zucchini, grated

1   Preheat the oven to 350°F. Line an 8" × 8" baking dish with parchment paper.

2   In a large bowl, mix together the almond butter, egg, salt, baking soda, sugar, and vanilla until well combined. Fold in the chocolate chips and zucchini. Pour into the prepared dish, pressing down to spread evenly.

3   Bake for 25 to 30 minutes, or until golden brown and a toothpick comes out clean. Let cool slightly before serving.

FUDGY PEANUT BUTTER BROWNIES WITH CARAMEL SAUCE

MAKES: about 12 // **COOK TIME:** 30 minutes

Jay was the inspiration for these brownies since his weakness is anything with chocolate peanut butter. The brown rice flour makes them gooey (don't swap it for a different flour—it won't be nearly as good) and you get hints of peanut butter, plus actual peanuts. Make it with creamy peanut butter if you don't want chunks of peanuts in your brownies. Doesn't matter, creamy or chunky, and I'm lucky to see these still around 2 days later.

⅓ cup coconut oil, melted + more for the pan

2 eggs

½ cup chunky peanut butter

¾ cup coconut sugar

1 cup plain Almond Milk (page 216)

½ teaspoon baking powder

¼ teaspoon pink Himalayan salt

½ cup raw cocoa powder

1 cup oat flour

½ cup brown rice flour

½ cup dark chocolate chips, divided

Caramel Sauce (page 232)

1   Preheat the oven to 350°F. Grease a 9" × 9" baking dish with coconut oil.

2   In a large bowl, whisk together the eggs, peanut butter, sugar, milk, baking powder, salt, cocoa powder, and ⅓ cup oil. Add the oat and rice flours and mix until well combined. Fold in ¼ cup of the chocolate chips.

3   Pour the batter into the prepared baking dish, using a spatula to spread it evenly and smooth out the surface. Top with the remaining ¼ cup chocolate chips. Bake for 25 to 30 minutes, or until a toothpick comes out clean. Let cool before cutting into squares. Serve with Caramel Sauce drizzled over top.

NO-BAKE CAKE BALLS

MAKES: about 18 // **TOTAL TIME:** 1 hour 15 minutes

I know what you're thinking: There's no way these really taste like cake. But trust me, they *do*. These are the perfect little treats to have on hand for when you just want a little something. I find myself going back to the fridge three or four times to pop another in my mouth, they're so good. Plus, my kids go nuts for these, and I have peace of mind knowing they're made with good ingredients.

⅓ cup coconut flour

1⅓ cups almond flour

5 tablespoons pure maple syrup

2 teaspoons pure vanilla extract

¼ cup coconut oil, melted

¼ cup plain Almond Milk (page 216)

Pinch of pink Himalayan salt

¼ cup raw turbinado sugar

1   Line a large baking sheet with parchment paper.

2   In a medium bowl, combine coconut and almond flours, maple syrup, vanilla, oil, milk, and salt until well combined. Using your hands, roll the dough into marble-size balls.

3   Pour the sugar in a small bowl. Roll each dough ball in the sugar to coat, then place on the baking sheet. Place in the freezer and chill for at least 1 hour or up to overnight. Will keep well in the fridge for up to 2 weeks or the freezer for up to a month.

PUDDING POPS

MAKES: 6 // **COOK TIME:** 5 minutes

These remind me of the Fudgsicles I ate growing up. So good. Here's the only thing: Not all gelatin is created equal. I prefer Great Lakes because of the quality, but you have to use more of it than normal gelatin. If using generic gelatin, try 1 tablespoon instead of 2. You may have to play around with this until you reach the perfect fudgy consistency. I made them one time using 1½ tablespoons generic gelatin and they were legit pudding, which is still good, but ideally they should be fudgy and melt in your mouth.

---

1 cup canned full-fat coconut milk

1 tablespoon raw cocoa powder

2 tablespoons pure maple syrup

Pink Himalayan salt

2 tablespoons Great Lakes Gelatin (you may only need 1 tablespoon if using a different brand)

1   In a medium saucepan over medium-high heat, bring the milk, cocoa powder, maple syrup, and a pinch of salt to a boil. While whisking, add the gelatin and whisk for 1 minute, making sure to get out any clumps. Remove from the heat.

2   For best results, cool the mixture in an ice bath before freezing: Put a couple of handfuls of ice in a large bowl with ½ cup water. Pour the mixture in a medium bowl and place on top of the ice. Continuously whisk until warm to the touch.

3   Evenly pour the mixture into popsicle molds or paper cups with a popsicle stick placed in each. Freeze for at least 3 hours or up to overnight. Keeps well in the freezer for up to 3 weeks.

CLASSIC CHOCOLATE CHIP COOKIES

MAKES: about 50 // **COOK TIME:** 40 minutes

My mom and I made chocolate chip cookies together all the time when I was young. We always made a huge batch and froze about half. Today, I still do the same because it just wouldn't be right if I didn't make a million and have some in the freezer. I actually like the cookies better frozen. These are a great hostess gift, and the recipe makes so many that you can keep some for yourself (no one will ever know).

2¼ cups oat flour

1 teaspoon baking soda

1 teaspoon pink Himalayan salt

2 sticks butter, softened

1½ cups coconut sugar

1 teaspoon pure vanilla extract

2 eggs

1 cup dark chocolate chips

1 Preheat the oven to 375°F. Line 3 large baking sheets with parchment paper.

2 In a large bowl, mix the flour, baking soda, and salt until combined.

3 In a medium bowl, using an electric mixer, beat the butter and sugar together. Add the vanilla and eggs, one at a time, until combined. Add the mixture to the bowl with the dry ingredients and mix well. Fold in the chocolate chips.

4 Spoon small dollops of batter onto the prepared baking sheets, making sure to leave a little space in between each cookie. Bake for 15 to 18 minutes, or until golden brown. Transfer to cooling racks and let cool completely.

FLOURLESS CASHEW BUTTER COOKIES

MAKES: about 30 // **COOK TIME:** 10 minutes

These cookies are beautifully simple yet strangely addictive, and are a nice change from the typical almond butter cookies. Moist, delicious, and not overly sweet, these can be served with coffee as a light afternoon treat or dessert.

1 jar (12 ounces) creamy cashew butter

½ cup coconut sugar

2 large eggs

½ teaspoon vanilla extract

½ teaspoon baking soda

¼ teaspoon pink Himalayan salt

1 Preheat the oven to 350°F. Line a large baking sheet with parchment paper.

2 In a large bowl, mix the cashew butter, sugar, eggs, vanilla, baking soda, and salt until combined. The dough will be very sticky.

3 Spoon the dough by tablespoon onto the prepared baking sheet, evenly spacing them out. Press down the top of each cookie with the back of a spoon or your finger, or make a crisscross with a fork. Bake for 8 to 10 minutes, or until golden brown.

4 Remove from the oven and let cool on the baking sheet for 5 minutes before transferring to a cooling rack to cool completely.

CLASSIC CHOCOLATE SOUFFLÉ

SERVES: 6 // **COOK TIME:** 25 minutes

I would argue that soufflés aren't bad for you since they're mostly just eggs, right? Okay, a little sugar, but there are worse things out there. I'm half kidding. But honestly, don't be scared to make soufflés because you've "heard" they are one of the hardest things to make. The hardest part is that they're slightly time-consuming. The first time I made these was for Jay in 2012, and I remember being thrilled that they didn't fall flat. If I could do it back then, you can do it, too.

**2 tablespoons butter +
more for the ramekins**

**½ cup coconut sugar,
divided + more for the
ramekins**

**1 cup dark chocolate
chips**

**1 teaspoon vanilla
extract**

**¼ teaspoon pink
Himalayan salt**

3 large egg yolks

6 large egg whites

1 Preheat the oven to 375°F. Butter 6 ramekins and coat each with sugar.

2 Using a bain-marie method (see note below) or a double boiler, melt the chocolate chips and 2 tablespoons butter together, stirring occasionally, until completely smooth. Remove from the heat and stir in the vanilla and salt. Let cool for 5 to 8 minutes, or until warm to the touch.

3 In a large bowl, whisk the egg yolks with ¼ cup of the sugar for 2 minutes, or until light in color and ribbons form. Fold the chocolate mixture into the egg yolks until completely combined.

4 In a medium bowl, beat the egg whites for 5 minutes, or until fluffy and medium-soft peaks form. Add the remaining ¼ cup sugar and beat for 5 minutes, or until stiff peaks form. Fold the whites into the chocolate mixture, ¼ cup at a time, until well combined. Be sure not to stir to lose fluffiness.

5 Divide the mixture among the ramekins. Bake for 18 to 20 minutes, or until a toothpick comes out clean and the soufflé has risen. Serve immediately.

Note: To melt the chips using the bain-marie method, place the chocolate chips and 2 tablespoons butter in a glass or other heatproof bowl. Place the bowl over a pot of simmering water (a bain-marie) and allow the chocolate to completely melt, stirring occasionally.

LEMON CUSTARD CAKES

SERVES: 8 // **COOK TIME:** 35 minutes

This little creation was a mistake that ended up being quite possibly the best thing to ever happen—it's probably my favorite dessert. It was supposed to be lemon bars but accidentally became a moist, delicious cake. The crust is the same recipe as the chocolate chip cookies sans chocolate chips. Paired with the zesty, sweet lemon topping, it's any lemon-tart/key-lime-pie-lover's jam. Even my "I hate anything lemon" husband gets after this concoction. If you don't have 8 ramekins, use a greased 8" x 8" baking dish, but be prepared to eat it right out of the pan with a spoon (it's too moist to cut bars out). I've done it many times.

CRUST

Coconut oil, for the ramekins

1 cup + 2 tablespoons oat flour

½ teaspoon baking soda

½ teaspoon pink Himalayan salt

1 stick butter, at room temperature

¾ cup coconut sugar

½ teaspoon pure vanilla extract

1 egg

LEMON TOPPING

6 eggs

1 cup raw honey

4 teaspoons lemon zest

1 cup fresh lemon juice

¼ cup almond flour

1   *To make the crust:* Preheat the oven to 375°F. Grease 8 small ramekins with coconut oil.

2   In a large bowl, mix the flour, baking soda, and salt until combined. In a medium bowl, using an electric mixer, beat the butter and sugar together. Add the vanilla and egg until combined. Add the wet ingredients to the dry ingredients and mix well.

3   Using your finger, smooth about 2 tablespoons of the batter on the bottom and three-quarters of the way up the sides of each ramekin until ⅛" thick. Bake for 12 to 15 minutes, or until golden brown. Let cool 20 minutes.

4   *To make the lemon topping:* In another large bowl, whisk together the eggs, honey, lemon zest and juice, and flour until smooth and well combined. Pour the mixture evenly over the cooled crusts until almost completely full. Reduce the oven to 350°F and bake for 18 minutes, or until the mixture sets up.

5   Let cool on the counter for 15 to 20 minutes, then place in the refrigerator, covered, for at least 2 hours or up to overnight. Keeps well on the counter for a day or in the fridge for up to a week.

GRANDMA'S APPLE PIE

SERVES: 6–8 // **COOK TIME:** 1 hour 10 minutes

I can only imagine how proud my grandma would have been (if she was still around) to see that I have a cookbook and that her (updated) recipe for apple pie is included. Full Italian, she was tiny and petite, but strong and sharp as nails—and, wow, could she cook. She made the best gnocco fritto (or as we called it, pizza-freit, better known as fried dough . . . um, yeah, so good) and apple pie. Her apple pie is the best because it's simple. No need to add a bunch of fluff to a recipe that only needs a little butter to make it the best. I swapped my grandma's white flour for healthier oat and almond flours and would argue it tastes just as good. Grandma would approve.

CRUST

2 cups blanched almond flour

1½ cups oat flour

1 cup arrowroot powder

½ cup coconut sugar

1 teaspoon pink Himalayan salt

3 eggs

⅔ cup cold butter, cut into ½" cubes

OAT LAYER

½ cup old-fashioned rolled oats

¼ cup shredded coconut

¼ cup coconut sugar

3 tablespoons butter, melted

1   *To make the crust:* In a large bowl, mix the almond and oat flours, arrowroot powder, coconut sugar, and salt until combined. Add eggs, one at a time, and 4 tablespoons water. Using your hands, cut the butter into the dough until it's incorporated and only small pebble-size balls of butter are left. Turn onto a floured surface and knead the dough until it comes together (dough will be a little sticky). Form two equal-size balls and wrap each in plastic wrap. Chill in the fridge for at least 1 hour or up to overnight.

2   *To make the oat layer:* Meanwhile, preheat the oven to 350°F. In a shallow pan, mix the oats, shredded coconut, coconut sugar, and butter. Bake for 20 minutes, or until golden brown. Set aside.

3   Remove one dough ball from the fridge. Roll out on a floured surface until dough is ⅛" thick. Press the dough into an 8" pie dish. Using a knife or fork, liberally poke holes in the crust and trim off the excess.

4   Press the toasted oats on top of the crust in a thin layer, making sure to go up the sides as well. Chill in the fridge for at least 30 minutes or up to overnight.

APPLE FILLING

4–5 large Granny Smith apples, cored, sliced very thin, and halved

Pink Himalayan salt

¾ cup coconut sugar

¼ cup butter

¼ teaspoon ground nutmeg

½ teaspoon ground cinnamon

2 tablespoons arrowroot powder

5   *To make the apple filling:* In a large skillet over medium heat, sauté the apple slices and a small pinch of salt for 5 minutes, or until you start to see some juices. Add the sugar, butter, nutmeg, cinnamon, arrowroot powder, and ¼ cup water and cook for 5 minutes, or until the apples are tender and everything is well combined and slightly thickened. Pour into the pie dish over the oats.

6   Preheat the oven to 350°F. Roll out the other dough ball following the same instructions in step 3. Once rolled out, gently place on top of the pie. Press down on the sides and trim the excess. Poke a few small holes around the top, or cut one big hole in the middle. Bake for 35 to 40 minutes, or until golden brown.

RASPBERRY-ORANGE GUMMIES

MAKES: about 40 // **COOK TIME:** 10 minutes

My kids go bonkers for these, and I don't have to worry about any crazy additives. The boys even like them in their lunches at school—that's how I know they're good. I love Great Lakes Gelatin because of how clean it is, but if you use another brand, you may find you don't need to use as much gelatin (more generic brands are typically stronger). Start by using 2 tablespoons gelatin, then increasing if needed.

¾ cup orange juice

1½ cups raspberries

¼ cup raw honey

¼ cup Great Lakes Gelatin (you may only need 2 tablespoons if using a different brand)

1   Place the orange juice and raspberries in a high-powered blender. Blend on high until completely smooth. Pour into a small saucepan over medium heat. Add the honey and stir to combine.

2   Add the gelatin, whisking continuously, and bring the mixture to a boil. Reduce the heat to low and continue whisking for 5 minutes, or until everything is incorporated and the mixture thickens slightly. Remove from the heat.

3   Pour into an 8" × 8" baking dish or silicone mold of choice. Place in the refrigerator for at least 1 hour, or until completely firmed up.

4   Remove from the baking dish and cut into bite-size gummies.

BROWN VANILLA CUPCAKE WITH CHOCOLATE COCONUT CREAM

MAKES: 12 // **COOK TIME:** 20 minutes

There's just something about a classic vanilla cupcake with chocolate frosting that gets me. I like traditional flavors and don't want to fix anything that isn't broken. These cupcakes get their brownish color—and the most amazing vanilla flavor—from the vanilla bean powder. I could eat all 12 of these cupcakes they're so moist, fluffy, and light. Just wait to frost them until you're ready to eat them (and they are completely cooled) because the frosting will seep into the cupcakes the longer it sits (fresh coconut cream is delicious and good for you, but it won't stay looking pretty for too long).

1¼ cups oat flour

1¼ teaspoons baking powder

½ teaspoon baking soda

½ teaspoon pink Himalayan salt

¾ cup coconut sugar

2 teaspoons vanilla bean powder

½ cup Cashew Milk (page 217)

3 eggs

½ cup coconut oil, melted

Chocolate Coconut Cream (page 213)

1   Preheat the oven to 350°F. Line a muffin pan with muffin liners.

2   In a large bowl, stir together the flour, baking powder, baking soda, salt, sugar, and vanilla powder until combined.

3   In a medium bowl, whisk together the milk, eggs, and oil. Pour into the dry ingredients and stir to combine. Spoon the batter into the muffin liners, filling each until almost full. Bake for 18 to 20 minutes, or until a toothpick comes out clean. Let cool completely.

4   Once cool, spread about 1 tablespoon Chocolate Coconut Cream on each cupcake. Enjoy right away or keep in an airtight container for up to 5 days.

CHOCOLATE COCONUT CREAM

MAKES: about 1 cup // **TOTAL TIME:** 2 hours 5 minutes

1 can (13.5 ounces) full-fat coconut milk

1 tablespoon pure maple syrup

1 teaspoon pure vanilla extract

1 teaspoon raw cacao powder

1   Place the can of coconut milk upside down in the refrigerator for at least 2 hours or up to overnight. This is to harden and separate the cream.

2   Take the can out of the fridge, open, and scoop the coconut cream and 2 tablespoons of the liquid into a medium bowl, discarding the rest of the liquid (or save it for smoothies!). Add the maple syrup, vanilla and cacao. Whisk, breaking up coconut milk pieces, for 1 minute, or until the mixture slightly thickens. Use immediately or store in fridge for 3 to 4 days.

CASHEW CREAM

MAKES: about 1 cup // **TOTAL TIME:** 4 hours 10 minutes

1 cup cashews, soaked at least 4 hours, rinsed and drained

3 tablespoons pure maple syrup

¼ cup plain Almond Milk (page 216) or Cashew Milk (page 217)

1 teaspoon vanilla bean powder

In a high-powdered blender, place the cashews, maple syrup, milk, and vanilla powder. Blend on high for 1 to 2 minutes, or until smooth. Use right away or store in an airtight container for up to 5 days in the fridge.

STAPLES

PLAIN AND VANILLA ALMOND MILK

MAKES: about 4 cups // **TOTAL TIME:** 8 hours 5 minutes

I've been making almond milk for years—my dad taught me when I was in my early twenties. Since then, I've never looked back. I love knowing there aren't any additives in my milk, and my digestive system and skin appreciate the dairy-free alternative. Depending on what I'll be using the milk for, I'll either leave it plain (just almonds blended up with water) or add maple syrup, vanilla, even cinnamon or nutmeg. Lattes made with fresh almond milk are my weakness.

1 cup raw almonds, soaked 8 hours or up to overnight

2 tablespoons pure maple syrup (optional)

½ teaspoon pure vanilla powder, for the vanilla version

Drain and rinse the almonds. Place in a high-powered blender with 4 cups filtered water and maple syrup and vanilla (if using). Blend on high for 1 to 2 minutes. In a large bowl, strain the milk using a nut bag or cheesecloth. Discard the pulp. Store in a glass jar in the fridge for 5 to 7 days.

CASHEW MILK

MAKES: about 4 cups // **TOTAL TIME:** 8 hours 5 minutes

Cashew milk is my favorite kitchen discovery as of late. This thick, creamy concoction can emulate any type of milk (from skim to whole) and be even creamier, depending on how much water you use. Using 3 cups of water will yield results that resemble whole milk, so add more water to thin out, or use about 1½ cups water for a thick creamer. And you don't have to strain cashew milk like other nut milks. Yas!

1 cup raw cashews, soaked for 8 hours or up to overnight

2 tablespoons pure maple syrup (optional)

1 teaspoon pure vanilla extract (optional)

Drain and rinse the cashews. Place in a high-powered blender with 3 cups filtered water and maple syrup and vanilla (if using). Blend on high for 1 to 2 minutes. Store in a glass jar in the fridge for 5 to 7 days.

CACAO CASHEW MILK

MAKES: about 4 cups // **TOTAL TIME:** 10 minutes

My pregnancies were all relatively boring in the sense that I never had any random food cravings. Out of all three pregnancies, I only had one moment when I needed something "that exact second" and that was thick, delicious chocolate milk. Jay ran out to get some, and I drank almost the entire bottle the moment I got my hands on it. I woke up the next morning with a rash (thanks, casein sensitivity) and never had it again. Had I discovered cashew milk back then (much thicker and creamier than almond milk), I would have been able to have that heavenly chocolate milk every single day. Oh well, better late than never.

---

4 cups Cashew Milk (page 217)

2 tablespoons raw cacao powder

Pinch of pink Himalayan salt

2–3 tablespoons pure maple syrup

Place the milk, cacao powder, salt, and maple syrup in a high-powered blender. Blend on high until well combined. Store in a glass container. It will last for 5 to 7 days in the fridge.

PECAN OR HAZELNUT MILK

MAKES: about 4 cups // **TOTAL TIME:** 3 hours 5 minutes for Pecan Milk, or 8 hours 5 minutes for Hazelnut Milk

These nut milk varieties have a distinct pecan or hazelnut flavor and aren't as thick as cashew or almond milk. But they are perfect for changing things up with their decadent flavor. Depending on what I'll be using the milk for, I'll either make it plain, which is blending the nuts with just water (ideal for smoothies), or I'll add maple syrup and vanilla to sweeten it up (perfect for coffee drinks).

1 cup raw pecans, soaked for 3 hours, or raw hazelnuts, soaked for 8 hours

2 tablespoons pure maple syrup (optional)

½ teaspoon pure vanilla extract (optional)

Drain and rinse the nuts. Place in a high-powered blender with 3 cups filtered water and maple syrup and vanilla (if using). Blend on high for 1 to 2 minutes. In a large bowl, strain the milk using a nut bag or cheesecloth. Discard the pulp. Store in a glass jar in the fridge for 5 to 7 days.

CHIPOTLE RANCH DRESSING

MAKES: almost 2 cups // **TOTAL TIME:** 10 minutes

This ranch is similar to the one in my first book, *Balancing in Heels*, but with a kick. It's perfect on salads, for dipping veggies, or even with wings. You will never go back to the bottled stuff again! Leave out the chipotle if you don't want it spicy. I use vegan mayo for the slightly blander taste, but feel free to use regular mayo.

1½ cups vegan mayonnaise

¼ cup plain Almond Milk (page 216)

1 tablespoon apple cider vinegar

1 tablespoon fresh chopped parsley

1½ teaspoons onion powder

1 teaspoon garlic powder

1–2 chipotle chile peppers in adobo sauce, depending on how spicy you like it (be careful when handling)

¼ teaspoon ground black pepper

½ teaspoon dried dill

In a high-powered blender, combine the mayo, milk, vinegar, parsley, onion powder, garlic powder, chile pepper, black pepper, and dill until creamy. Keeps well in the fridge for up to 10 days.

BASIC PICKLE RECIPE

MAKES: about 8 // **COOK TIME:** 10 minutes

Some store-bought pickles contain added colors and preservatives. No thanks. These are as healthy as you can get—pure, wholesome pickles made from real ingredients in your own kitchen. There's just something so satisfying about that yummy crunch of a pickle.

2 cups white wine vinegar

¼ cup raw honey

3 teaspoons pink Himalayan salt

1 teaspoon brown mustard seeds

½ teaspoon black peppercorns

1 bay leaf

1 sprig thyme

½ teaspoon fennel seeds

¾ teaspoon dill seeds

1–1½ pounds mini cucumbers

⅓ cup coarsely chopped dill

3 cloves garlic, roughly chopped

1 In a medium saucepan over medium-high heat, stir together the vinegar, honey, salt, mustard seeds, peppercorns, bay leaf, thyme, fennel seeds, dill seeds, and 4 cups water. Bring to a boil, then remove from the heat.

2 Pack the cucumbers into a large mason jar. Add the chopped dill and garlic. Pour the hot vinegar mixture over the cucumbers and cover.

3 Let cool to room temperature before storing in the refrigerator. Will last up to a month. For best results, wait 2 days before eating.

ROASTED GARLIC

MAKES: 1 // **COOK TIME:** 35 minutes

Roasted garlic is my favorite thing in the entire world. I eat whole cloves right out of the fridge. They are always good to have on hand since they make every recipe more flavorful with their rich, nutty notes.

---

1 head garlic

Extra virgin olive oil

Coarse sea salt

1   Preheat the oven to 400°F.

2   Cut the top off the head of garlic and peel away the outer layer. Drizzle with olive oil and sprinkle with one big pinch of salt. Wrap the garlic in foil, leaving a small hole so heat can escape. Bake for 35 minutes.

3   Let cool slightly, then squeeze out the garlic and mash it, or keep it whole. Keeps well in olive oil for up to a week in the fridge.

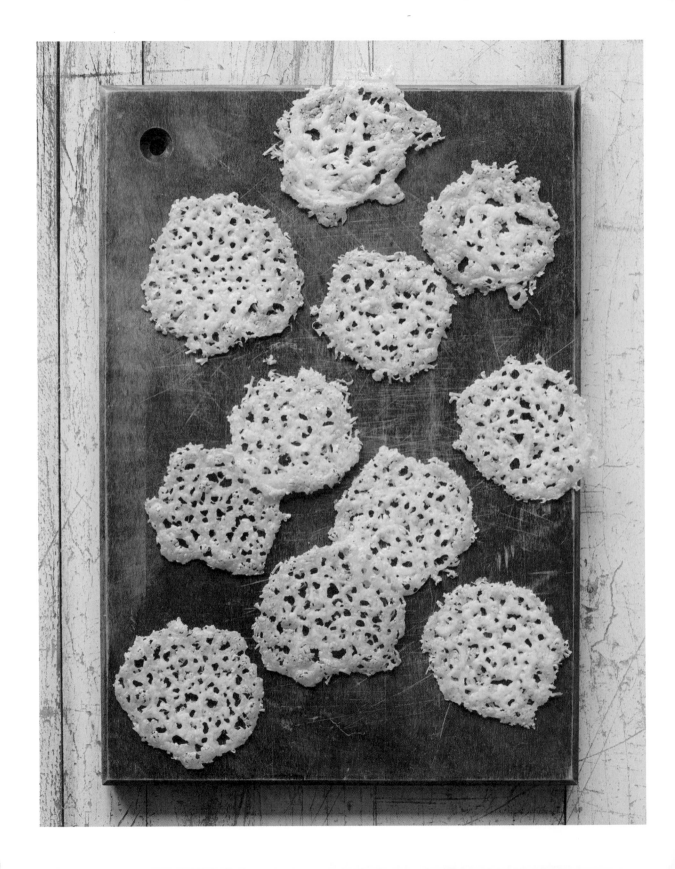

MANCHEGO CRISPS

MAKES: 4 // **COOK TIME:** 10 minutes

Have you ever ordered a salad at a restaurant and it came with one of those fancy cheese crisps that you kept dreaming about long after your meal was over? Well, here you go! Now you can re-create them in your kitchen—but let me warn you, they are addicting! Any hard cheese will work for this, but I prefer Manchego for its Parmesan flavor (plus it's made from sheep's milk). The crisps are pliable immediately after you remove them from the oven, so if you want to roll them up or make a fun crisp shape, that's the time to do it.

2 cups finely shredded Manchego cheese, divided

1   Preheat the oven to 375°F. Line a baking sheet with parchment paper.

2   Place $1/2$ cup of the cheese on the parchment and evenly spread out until it's 3" in diameter. Repeat with the remaining cheese. Bake for 10 minutes, or until golden brown. Let cool 2 to 3 minutes. The crisps will harden as they cool.

EVERYDAY KETCHUP

MAKES: about 2½ cups // **COOK TIME:** 30 minutes

Do you need to make your own ketchup? No, you can find decent ketchups out there without any harmful additives. However, homemade ketchup really does taste much better. It's fresh, light, and packed with flavor. It makes a big batch and will last up to a month.

1 can (28 ounces) peeled tomatoes

1 can (6 ounces) tomato paste

2 tablespoons blackstrap molasses

½ teaspoon garlic powder

½ teaspoon onion powder

⅛ teaspoon ground allspice

½ tablespoon Worcestershire sauce

¼ cup apple cider vinegar

Pink Himalayan salt

1   In a blender, add the tomatoes and blend on high until pureed. Place them in a medium saucepan over medium-high heat and bring to a boil.

2   Add the tomato paste and molasses and simmer for 5 minutes. Stir in the garlic powder, onion powder, allspice, Worcestershire sauce, and vinegar. Cook for 20 minutes, or until the mixture thickens. Season with salt and remove from the heat.

3   Let cool in the refrigerator for 1 hour before serving. The ketchup will thicken slightly as it cools.

STONE-GROUND MUSTARD

MAKES: about 1 cup // **TOTAL TIME:** 2 days 15 minutes

You don't need to make your own mustard, but it's well worth it. You can really taste the creamy, bold flavor. The mustard might be a little spicy at first, but that should lessen after a few days.

3 tablespoons yellow mustard seeds

3 tablespoons brown mustard seeds

⅓ cup dark beer

⅓ cup apple cider vinegar

1 tablespoon raw honey

1 small clove garlic

¼ teaspoon ground nutmeg

4 black peppercorns

¼ teaspoon pink Himalayan salt

1   Place the yellow and brown mustard seeds in a medium glass bowl. Add the beer, vinegar, honey, garlic, nutmeg, and peppercorns and stir to combine. Let sit in refrigerator, covered, for 48 hours.

2   Once the mustard seeds have soaked up most of the liquid, place in a high-powered blender with the salt. Blend to desired consistency. The mustard will last for up to a month.

SIMPLE GUACAMOLE

MAKES: about 1½ cups // **TOTAL TIME:** 10 minutes

Sometimes less is more, and that's the case with my simple guac, made with just a few beloved ingredients. A little lime and salt go a long way, and the jalapeño gives the right heat.

3 avocados, peeled, pit removed

½ teaspoon coarse sea salt

½ large lime, juiced

1 teaspoon minced jalapeño chile pepper (be careful when handling)

In a large bowl, place the avocados, salt, lime, and chile pepper. Mash with a fork until only a few small chunks remain, or to your desired consistency. Serve with chips or use for tacos or whatever you like!

FIRE-ROASTED SALSA

MAKES: about 5 cups // **COOK TIME:** 12 minutes

Fresh, with a charred flavor, this salsa is perfect with the simple guac and chips. Make the Fizzy Spicy Margaritas (page 182) and you have yourself a delightful little evening.

2 pounds roma tomatoes

1 jalapeño chile pepper, halved and seeds removed (be careful when handling)

1 red bell pepper, halved

2 cloves garlic

½ red onion, sliced

¼ cup olive oil

Pink Himalayan salt

½ teaspoon ground cumin

½ teaspoon chili powder

½ lime, juiced

½ bunch cilantro with stems

1 Heat the grill or a grill pan over high heat.

2 On a large baking sheet, spread out the tomatoes, chile pepper, bell pepper, garlic, and onion. Coat with the oil and season with salt.

3 Place the veggies on the grill pan or directly on the grill. Grill the vegetables on each side for 12 minutes total, or until black and charred, pulling off the veggies as they become really charred (about 1–2 minutes for garlic, 5–8 minutes for the chile pepper, 8–9 minutes for the onion, and 10–12 minutes for the tomatoes and bell pepper). Place the vegetables back on the baking sheet.

4 In a blender or food processor, add the charred vegetables, cumin, chili powder, lime juice, and cilantro. Blend or process until the mixture becomes a smooth consistency. Serve warm or let cool in the refrigerator for at least 1 hour.

ROASTED CORN SALSA

MAKES: about 1 cup // **COOK TIME:** 10 minutes

One of my favorite things about summer is fresh corn. It can be tough sometimes to find non-GMO corn, but luckily it's becoming more readily available. Put this on tacos or a salad, or use it as a dip for chips.

2 cups corn

½ cup halved cherry tomatoes

1 tablespoon chopped shallots

1 tablespoon chopped parsley

½ teaspoon smoked paprika

1 teaspoon white wine vinegar

⅛ teaspoon chili powder

1 teaspoon lemon zest

1 teaspoon olive oil

Pink Himalayan salt

Ground black pepper

1   Preheat the oven to 450°F.

2   Place the corn on a small baking sheet and roast for 10 minutes, or until golden brown.

3   Place in a medium bowl. Add the cherry tomatoes, shallots, parsley, paprika, vinegar, chili powder, lemon zest, and oil. Stir until combined. Add salt and pepper to taste. Let chill for at least 1 hour or up to overnight.

CARAMEL SAUCE

MAKES: about 2 cups // **COOK TIME:** 35 minutes

Caramel sauce is typically made with milk and white sugar, a definite no-no for me and my family. But what is life without some caramel sauce? I had to have it, but in my own way. Thank goodness for coconut sugar and coconut milk. If you'd rather create frozen caramel pops, then add 2 tablespoons arrowroot powder, pour the mixture into popsicle molds, and freeze for at least 3 hours!

½ cup coconut sugar

1 tablespoon arrowroot powder

1 can (13.5 ounces) full-fat coconut milk

1 teaspoon pure vanilla extract

1 In a medium saucepan, bring the sugar and ¼ cup water to a boil.

2 In a small bowl, dissolve the arrowroot powder in 1 tablespoon water. Add to the saucepan, along with the milk. Reduce the heat to a simmer and cook, whisking occasionally, for 30 to 35 minutes, or until slightly thickened. Remove from the heat and stir in the vanilla.

3 Place in a mason jar, cover, and refrigerate for 3 hours or up to overnight. The caramel will significantly thicken as it chills. Keeps well in the fridge for up to 10 days.

AIOLI

If I could only make one "condiment" for the rest of my life, it would be aioli—there's nothing like this fresh, homemade flavor. Smear aioli on the bottom of your plate, place a piece of fish or meat on top, sprinkle on some micro-greens, and you have yourself a picture-worthy meal. I love the Simple Aioli (page 233) for grilled proteins, such as lamb and roasted veggies. The Roasted Garlic Aioli (page 234) is delicious on a roast beef sandwich or with seafood, such as scallops or salmon. The Spicy Miso Aioli (page 234) goes perfectly with seafood. And the Sun-Dried Tomato and Herb Aioli (page 235) is amazing with chicken or as a dip for crudités. Just make sure not to use extra virgin olive oil. Reach for a light olive oil instead, because extra virgin will leave a slightly bitter taste in your mouth.

SIMPLE AIOLI

MAKES: about 1 cup // **TOTAL TIME:** 25 minutes

2 egg yolks

1 teaspoon Dijon mustard

¼ teaspoon fresh lemon juice

1 cup light olive oil

2 teaspoons champagne vinegar, divided

Pink Himalayan salt

1 Place a dish towel on the countertop to prevent the bowl from moving.

2 Place a large bowl on top of the towel. Add the egg yolks, mustard, and lemon juice and whisk to combine. Slowly drizzle in the oil, whisking vigorously for 2 to 3 minutes, or until completely combined and the mixture thickens substantially. Add the vinegar and salt to taste and whisk to combine (the aioli will lighten in color).

3 Place in the fridge for 15 to 20 minutes before serving.

ROASTED GARLIC AIOLI

MAKES: about 1 cup // **TOTAL TIME:** 25 minutes

4–8 cloves Roasted
Garlic (page 223),
depending how much
garlic you want

2 egg yolks

1 teaspoon Dijon
mustard

¼ teaspoon fresh lemon
juice

1 cup light olive oil

1 teaspoon champagne
vinegar

½ teaspoon
Worcestershire sauce

Pink Himalayan salt

Ground black pepper

1   Smash the garlic on a cutting board with the top of a knife to create a garlic paste.

2   Place a dish towel on the countertop to prevent the bowl from moving. Place a large bowl on top of the towel. Add the egg yolks, mustard, and lemon juice and whisk to combine. Slowly drizzle in the oil, whisking vigorously for 2 to 3 minutes, or until completely combined and the mixture thickens substantially. Add the vinegar, Worcestershire sauce, garlic, and salt and pepper to taste and whisk to combine (the aioli will lighten in color).

3   Place in the fridge for 15 to 20 minutes before serving.

SPICY MISO AIOLI

MAKES: about 1 cup // **TOTAL TIME:** 25 minutes

2 egg yolks

1 cup light olive oil

¼ teaspoon lime juice

1 teaspoon brown rice
vinegar

1 tablespoon red miso

2 teaspoons Sriracha
sauce

1   Place a dish towel on the countertop to prevent the bowl from moving.

2   Place a large bowl on top of the towel. Add the egg yolks and whisk to combine. Slowly drizzle in the oil, whisking vigorously for 2 to 3 minutes, or until completely combined and the mixture thickens substantially. Add the lime juice, vinegar, miso, and Sriracha and whisk to combine (the aioli will lighten in color).

3   Place in the fridge for 15 to 20 minutes before serving.

SUN-DRIED TOMATO AND HERB AIOLI

MAKES: about 1 cup // **TOTAL TIME:** 25 minutes

2 egg yolks

1 teaspoon Dijon mustard

1 cup light olive oil

2 tablespoons minced sun-dried tomatoes

1 teaspoon chopped basil

1 teaspoon chopped parsley

½ teaspoon chopped oregano

¼ teaspoon garlic powder

2 teaspoons red wine vinegar

Pink Himalayan salt

1 Place a dish towel on the countertop to prevent the bowl from moving.

2 Place a large bowl on top of the towel. Add the egg yolks and mustard and whisk to combine. Slowly drizzle in the oil, whisking vigorously for 2 to 3 minutes, or until completely combined and the mixture thickens substantially. Add the tomatoes, basil, parsley, oregano, garlic powder, vinegar, and salt to taste and whisk to combine (the aioli will lighten in color).

3 Place in the fridge for 15 to 20 minutes before serving.

INFUSED ICE CUBES

Infused ice cubes make me happy. Yes, I know how ridiculous that sounds, but it's true. I love them in my water on a hot summer day to infuse my drink with hints of ginger, mint, or whatever flavor I'm feeling like at the moment. They're fun in cocktails (see pages 182–191), especially when having friends over. And my kids think they're "cool" and enjoy eating them (hey, if they choose an ice cube over a lollipop, I would make these every damn day!). You can strain the mixture before freezing if you don't want little chunks in your drinks, but I prefer to leave the mint leaves (or ginger or lavender) in because they look more colorful and fun.

GINGER-INFUSED ICE CUBES

MAKES: about 18 // **COOK TIME**: 10 minutes

¼ **cup peeled and finely chopped fresh ginger**

1 In a medium saucepot, bring 3 cups filtered water and the ginger to a boil. Simmer for 10 minutes. Remove from the heat and let cool for 10 to 15 minutes.

2 Pour evenly into ice cube trays and place in the freezer for at least 1 hour before use. Will last in the freezer for up to a month.

MINT-INFUSED ICE CUBES

MAKES: about 18 // **COOK TIME:** 10 minutes

½ cup roughly chopped
fresh mint

1   In a medium saucepot, bring 3 cups filtered water and the mint to a boil. Simmer for 10 minutes. Remove from the heat and let cool for 10 to 15 minutes.

2   Pour evenly into ice cube trays and place in the freezer for at least 1 hour before use. Will last in the freezer for up to a month.

LAVENDER-LEMON-INFUSED ICE CUBES

MAKES: about 18 // **COOK TIME:** 10 minutes

2 lemons, zested

1 tablespoon fresh
lemon juice

1½ tablespoons culinary
lavender

1   In a medium saucepot, bring 3 cups filtered water, the lemon zest and juice, and lavender to a boil. Simmer for 10 minutes. Remove from the heat and let cool for 10 to 15 minutes.

2   Pour evenly into ice cube trays and place in the freezer for at least 1 hour before use. Will last in the freezer for up to a month.

INFUSED OLIVE OIL

When I have these oils on hand, I find they help with inspiration when I'm in a cooking rut. I base my meals on them, and without even realizing it, I've come up with something seemingly elaborate within seconds.

The chili oil is amazing on seafood such as crab or lobster and in any Asian dish as well as for sautéing veggies. The garlic oil is great to sear scallops in. I use the lemon oil for poaching fish and in lemon aioli. And the herb oil is perfect for chicken or tossing with pasta. Just make sure to store the oils in the fridge since the ingredients are cooked.

CHILI-INFUSED OLIVE OIL

MAKES: about 2 cups // **COOK TIME:** 10 minutes

2 cups olive oil

4 teaspoons crushed red-pepper flakes

1 In a small saucepot over low heat, combine the oil and pepper flakes. Cook for 10 minutes. Remove from the heat and let cool to room temperature.

2 Transfer the infused oil to a covered mason jar. The oil must be refrigerated and will last for up to a month. It will harden in the fridge, so let it warm to room temperature before using.

GARLIC-INFUSED OLIVE OIL

MAKES: about 2 cups // **COOK TIME:** 10 minutes

2 cups olive oil

5 cloves garlic, chopped

1 In a small saucepot over low heat, combine the oil and garlic. Cook for 10 minutes. Remove from the heat and let cool to room temperature.

2 Transfer the infused oil to a covered mason jar. The oil must be refrigerated and will last for up to a month. It will harden in the fridge, so let it warm to room temperature before using.

LEMON-INFUSED OLIVE OIL

MAKES: about 2 cups // **COOK TIME:** 10 minutes

2 cups olive oil

3 lemons, peeled

1 In a small saucepot over low heat, combine the oil and lemon peels (discard the lemons, or juice them and place in the fridge for another use). Cook for 10 minutes. Remove from the heat and let cool to room temperature.

2 Transfer the infused oil to a covered mason jar. The oil must be refrigerated and will last for up to a month. It will harden in the fridge, so let it warm to room temperature before using.

HERB-INFUSED OLIVE OIL

MAKES: about 2 cups // **COOK TIME:** 10 minutes

2 cups olive oil

2 sprigs rosemary

4 sprigs thyme

1 teaspoon dried basil

1 clove garlic

1 In a small saucepot over low heat, combine the oil, rosemary, thyme, basil, and garlic. Cook for 10 minutes. Remove from the heat and let cool to room temperature.

2 Transfer the infused oil to a covered mason jar. The oil must be refrigerated and will last for up to a month. It will harden in the fridge, so let it warm to room temperature before using.

SEASONED SALT

Use these salts to make everything a little easier—you can zone out and know the flavor will be there. The rosemary salt is great on chicken or lamb. The chili salt is heaven on sea bass, shrimp, or chicken. And the smoked salt is perfect for fish, chicken, veggies, or scallops.

ROSEMARY SEASONED SALT

MAKES: about 1 cup // **COOK TIME:** 25 minutes

1 cup coarse sea salt

3 tablespoons chopped fresh rosemary

1   Preheat the oven to 225°F. Line a small baking sheet with parchment paper.

2   In a small bowl, mix the salt and rosemary. Spread in an even layer on the prepared baking sheet. Bake for 25 minutes, or until dried out. Let cool slightly.

3   Place the seasoned salt in a food processor. Pulse a couple of times to combine, being careful not to grind it into powder. Transfer to a container. Will keep well for up to 2 months.

CHILI SEASONED SALT

MAKES: about 1 cup // **COOK TIME:** 25 minutes

1 cup coarse sea salt

3 tablespoons red-pepper flakes

1   Preheat the oven to 225°F. Line a small baking sheet with parchment paper.

2   In a small bowl, mix the salt and pepper flakes. Spread in an even layer on the prepared baking sheet. Bake for 25 minutes, or until dried out. Let cool slightly.

3   Place the seasoned salt in a food processor. Pulse a couple of times to combine, being careful not to grind it into powder. Transfer to a container. Will keep well for up to 2 months.

SMOKED SEASONED SALT

MAKES: about 1 cup // **COOK TIME:** 25 minutes

1 cup coarse sea salt

1 tablespoon smoked paprika

1 tablespoon liquid smoke

1   Preheat the oven to 225°F. Line a small baking sheet with parchment paper.

2   In a small bowl, mix the salt, paprika, and liquid smoke. Spread in an even layer on the prepared baking sheet. Bake for 25 minutes, or until dried out. Let cool slightly.

3   Place the seasoned salt in a food processor. Pulse a couple of times to combine, being careful not to grind it into powder. Transfer to a container. Will keep well for up to 2 months.

ACKNOWLEDGMENTS

Many, many thanks to the numerous people who helped make this cookbook come to life:

Most importantly, everyone at Rodale—Dervla, Rae Ann, Anna, Marilyn, Angie, Emily, and Susan—I can't thank you enough for making my dream become a reality. *True Roots* was such a passion project of mine and you gave me the opportunity to share my passion with the world.

Mike, I can't thank you enough for the countless hours we spent together in my kitchen. You taught me so much about flavors and cooking—those lessons are truly priceless. Thank you for taking a chance on me with this book and letting me learn and grow from your incredible culinary skills.

To the dream team who made this cookbook come to life: Kelsey Cherry, Robert Sesnek, Marwa Bashir, Dani Michelle, and Hannah Messinger. Bloomsbury Farm for the perfect hospitality. Tina Rupp, Carrie Purcell, and Stephanie Hanes for making my food look better than I ever could.

My family—Jay, Cam, Jax, and Saylor: Everything I do is for you guys. Thanks for unknowingly pushing me to be the best I can be.

Mom and Dad, I wouldn't be where I am without either of you. I am so thankful to you both for instilling very different qualities in me—all of which have made me who I am today.

Susan and Jack, thanks for always having my back and sticking with me through it all.

And last but not least, thank you to everyone who has supported me over the years. It's because of you guys I am able to live out a dream, and I will never take that for granted.

INDEX

Boldfaced page references indicate photographs.